Conduct Disorder and Offending Behaviour in Young People

Child and Adolescent Mental Health Series

Written for professionals and parents, these accessible, evidence-based resources are essential reading for anyone seeking to understand and promote children and young people's mental health. The work was commissioned by FOCUS, a multidisciplinary project based at the Royal College of Psychiatrists' Research Unit funded by the Gatsby Charitable Foundation. Each title in the series brings together practical and policy-level suggestions with up-to-the-minute analysis of research.

other books in the series

Understanding Attachment and Attachment Disorders
Theory, Evidence and Practice
Vivien Prior and Danya Glaser
ISBN 978 1 84310 245 8

Cannabis and Young People
Reviewing the Evidence
Richard Jenkins
ISBN 978 1 84310 398 1

Deliberate Self-Harm in Adolescence
Claudine Fox and Keith Hawton
ISBN 978 1 84310 237 3

Mental Health Services for Minority Ethnic Children and Adolescents
Edited by Mhemooda Malek and Carol Joughin
Foreword by Dr Kedar Nath Dwivedi
ISBN 978 1 84310 236 6

of related interest

Children and Behavioural Problems
Anxiety, Aggression, Depression and ADHD – A Biopsychological Model
with Guidelines for Diagnostics and Treatment
Martine F. Delfos
ISBN 978 1 84310 196 3

Conduct Disorder and Behavioural Parent Training
Research and Practice
Dermot O'Reilly
ISBN 978 1 84310 163 5

Children Who Commit Acts of Serious Interpersonal Violence
Messages for Best Practice
Edited by Ann Hagell and Renuka Jeyarajah-Dent
ISBN 978 1 84310 384 4

Child and Adolescent Mental Health Series

FOCUS

Conduct Disorder and Offending Behaviour in Young People

Findings from Research

Kristin Liabø
and Joanna Richardson

The Royal College of
Psychiatrists' Research and Training Unit

Jessica Kingsley Publishers
London and Philadelphia

Diagnostic Criteria from the *International Statistical Classification of Diseases and Related Health Problems: Tenth Revision* on pp.101–102 reproduced with permission from the World Health Organisation.

Diagnostic Criteria from the *Diagnostic and Statistical Manual of Mental Health Disorders* (fourth edition) on pp.102–103 reproduced with permission from the American Psychiatric Association.

First published in 2007
by Jessica Kingsley Publishers
116 Pentonville Road
London N1 9JB, UK
and
400 Market Street, Suite 400
Philadelphia, PA 19106, USA

www.jkp.com

Disclaimer
The opinions expressed in this book are those of the author (Joanna Richardson) and not necessarily of NICE.

Library of Congress Cataloging in Publication Data
A CIP catalog record for this book is available from the Library of Congress

British Library Cataloguing in Publication Data
A CIP catalogue record for this book is available from the British Library

ISBN 978 1 84310 508 4

Printed and bound in Great Britain by
Athenaeum Press, Gateshead, Tyne and Wear

Contents

Acknowledgements

Thanks are due to all the people who helped with this review. Carol Joughin initiated the work in her previous role at FOCUS. Angela Scott and Mervyn Townley assisted with the initial search strategies and sifting of papers. At the Child Health Research and Policy Unit, City University, we are indebted to Renee Kunkler and Julia Newbery who helped with the screening of search hits, referencing and critical appraisal. We are grateful to Nick Hindley and Helen Roberts who commented on an earlier draft. Several practitioners responded helpfully to our queries, in particular: Geoff Baruch and Charles Wells at the Brandon Centre, Dawn Walker at the Multidimensional Treatment Foster Care Team (North), Chris Mearns at the Chrysalis Fostering Project, and all those who replied to our call for topic suggestions. FOCUS would especially like to thank Sue Bailey who reviewed an earlier manuscript, and made astute suggestions, and Stephen Scott who advised on the pharmacological section.

Preface

> How could we stop the referral of a conduct-disordered adolescent being a heart-sink? (Consultant child and adolescent psychiatrist)

Although every young person will present a unique case, conclusions drawn from research of interventions conducted on similar populations may help professionals, who are working with these adolescents, make decisions that will make a real difference to the young people, their families and the communities in which they live.

This book focuses on conduct problems in adolescence. While by no means all young people with conduct disorders are in trouble with the law (or vice versa), there is an overlap with the youth offending population.

Media tends to portray youth offending behaviour as a problem for affected neighbours and communities, but it is also a serious problem for the young people involved. Behaviour problems and involvement in criminal activities have been linked to continuing offending, substance misuse, and lack of education and work, all factors associated with shorter life expectancy. In recent years, the impetus for preventive services in the 0–3 age group has manifested itself in the UK Children's Centres (previously Sure Start). This focus on prevention has strong research backing. At the same time, preventive services will not 'work' for every child. This book looks at interventions designed to reduce adolescent problem behaviour.

Children and young people are both victims and perpetrators of crime. In a survey by the Home Office, more than a third of children aged 10–15 had experienced at least one personal crime in the last 12 months (Wood 2005). Young people excluded from school, or whose siblings were in trouble with the police, were more likely to be victimised (NACRO 2004). In terms of detected crime, young people are more likely to offend than adults (NACRO 2004). Governmental initiatives to reduce youth offending include Youth Offender Panels, Anti-Social Behaviour Orders and Local Child Curfews. The Respect Action Plan (launched in January 2006) includes the extended application of parenting contracts. A key question related to any initiative is whether it will actually produce change in young people.

Alongside the implementation of the Every Child Matters agenda, there is a need for more research evidence on interventions for this group. Furthermore, we need to develop interventions that are appropriate to the cultural norms and characteristics of service users in the UK. Much of the literature presented here comes from the US, and as such, this review is better seen as an overview of intervention research findings rather than an evidence-based practice manual.

FOCUS, a project within the Royal College of Psychiatrists' Research and Training Unit, promotes effective, evidence-based practice in child and adolescent mental health services (CAMHS). FOCUS produces evidence-based publications which review the existing literature and critically appraise research in order to establish the quality of the research base with respect to different topic areas within CAMHS. Within FOCUS the College Research and Training Unit also coordinates the Quality Improvement Network for Multi-Agency CAMHS and provides training to the CAMHS workforce.

With this in mind, the main aim of this book is to provide a summary of the best available research evidence on interventions for young people with conduct disorder or involved in offending. It begins by defining the disorder, examines diagnoses that often occur alongside, and discusses risk factors. Research evidence related to the treatment of conduct disorder and interventions for young offenders is discussed in Part Two.

There is some overlap in the literature and in order to avoid repetitions, research that focuses both on offending and behaviour is presented under the chapters on conduct disorder. Research looking at criminal involvement only is presented in the chapter on offending.

Appendix 2 provides an overview of key terms in systematic reviewing, and this may assist readers who are new to research on the effectiveness of interventions.

Part One

Introduction

1 Overview of Conduct Disorder

Definitions and terminology

Conduct disorders are characterised by a repetitive and persistent pattern of antisocial, aggressive or defiant behaviour. Young people with conduct disorder may exhibit excessive levels of fighting or bullying; cruelty to animals or other people; severe destructiveness to property; firesetting; stealing; repeated lying; truancy from school and running away from home; unusually frequent and severe temper tantrums; and defiant provocative behaviour. The behaviours that are associated with conduct disorder are major violations of age-appropriate social expectations, and are more severe than ordinary childish mischief or adolescent rebelliousness (BMA Board of Science 2006). Isolated antisocial or criminal acts are not in themselves grounds for the diagnosis of conduct disorder, which requires an enduring pattern of a range of difficult behaviour of at least six months prior to diagnosis (see Appendix 1 for ICD-10 (WHO 1994) and DSM-IV (APA 1994) diagnostic criteria).

The diagnostic criteria for conduct disorder are similar but not identical to antisocial personality disorder. According to the *International Classification of Diseases* (ICD-10) (WHO 1994) and the *Diagnostic and Statistical Manual of Mental Disorders* (DSM-IV) (APA 1994), conduct disorder usually occurs during childhood or adolescence, whereas antisocial personality disorder is not diagnosed in people under the age of 18. Furthermore, according to ICD-10 and DSM-IV criteria, any diagnosis should distinguish between early-onset (symptoms present before the age of ten) and late-onset conduct disorder (absence of symptoms before the age of ten). The diagnostic criteria are also similar to oppositional defiant disorder

(ODD), which according to ICD-10 usually occurs in younger children and 'does not include delinquent acts or the more extreme forms of aggressive or dissocial behaviour' (WHO 1994). ODD is generally seen as milder than, and a risk factor to developing, conduct disorder.

Several terms have been used to describe conduct disorder, including antisocial behaviour, acting out, externalising behaviour, disruptive behaviour and conduct problems (Kazdin 1995). The diagnostic criteria described above have been criticised for ignoring the context in which antisocial behaviour and conduct problems occur. Considering the strong correlation between conduct disorder and social deprivation, this criticism is in many ways well-founded. The aetiology of conduct disorder is complex, and it can be argued that ICD-10 and DSM-IV fail to account for these complexities, including comorbidity. However, for research purposes, the diagnostic criteria are useful as a common language (Richters and Cicchetti 1993).

Offending behaviour often presents itself during the adolescent years. This may amount to no more than one or two incidents of shoplifting or graffiti, or it may escalate into persistent, and sometimes more serious, criminal behaviour. The Home Office has defined persistent young offenders as a person who is 'aged 10–17 who has been sentenced for one or more recordable offences on three or more separate occasions and is arrested again (or has an information laid against him or her) within three years of last being sentenced' (Home Office 1997).

Juvenile delinquency is a social, rather than a diagnostic, category that refers to children and adolescents who break the law. Delinquent behaviour may well lead to or be part of a diagnosis of conduct disorder, but not all children or adolescents who offend are conduct disordered. More research is needed on the link between youth crime and health. Services aimed at young offenders have tended to remain distinct from those provided by the health sector. Research looking at the prevalence of mental health problems in young offenders has reported high rates (Department of Health 2004; Hagell 2002). One UK study estimated that over 50 per cent of remanded young males and over 30 per cent of sentenced young males have a diagnosable disorder (Liddle 1999). Conduct and oppositional disorders are the most frequent diagnoses, and these often occur alongside attention-deficit disorders or depression (Hagell 2002). There are a number of behaviours that overlap with the formal conduct disorder diagnosis but the differences between those who are incarcerated and those who obtain treatment in mental health settings for conduct disorder may be small (Hagell 2002; Shamsie, Hamilton and Sykes 1996).

Prevalence

In the latter part of the last century there was a sharp increase in rates of antisocial disorder, suicidal behaviour, depressive disorder and substance abuse among young people (Rutter 1999). Conduct disorders are now the most prevalent mental health problem in young people. In a British survey of young people between the ages of 11 and 15 it was found that, overall, conduct disorders occur in 7 per cent of the population (up from 6.2% in 1999), affecting 8.1 per cent of males (8.6% in 1999) and 5.1 per cent of females (3.8% in 1999) (Green *et al.* 2005). Table 1.1 provides a breakdown of these prevalence figures by types of conduct disorder.

Table 1.1 Prevalence rates of conduct disorder in Great Britain for young people aged 11–15			
Type of conduct disorder	**Boys (%)**	**Girls (%)**	**All (%)**
Oppositional defiant disorder	3.5	1.7	5.2
Unsocialised conduct disorder	1.2	0.8	2.0
Socialised conduct disorder	2.6	1.9	4.5
Other conduct disorder	0.7	0.8	1.5

(Source: Green *et al.* 2005. Crown copyright 2005)

In general, children with conduct disorder were more likely to be living in social sector housing, with neither parent working, and where the interviewed parent had no educational qualifications. They were less likely to be living with married parents, and more likely to be living in a household with stepchildren (Green *et al.* 2005). Of all young people who present to child and adolescent mental health services (CAMHS) for treatment, it is estimated that between 40 per cent and 60 per cent had some form of disruptive, antisocial or aggressive behaviour (Audit Commission 1999).

Conduct disorder is particularly prevalent among young people in local authority care, and surveys have found clinical conduct disorder rates in this population to be 37 per cent in England, 36 per cent in Scotland, and 42 per cent in Wales (Meltzer *et al.* 2002, 2004a, 2004b). Conduct disorders appear to be more prevalent in young people placed in residential care (Meltzer *et al.* 2002).

Long-term outlook

There has been a growing awareness of the social and financial costs associated with a conduct disorder diagnosis (House of Commons Health Committee 1997; Scott *et al.* 2001). Main costs are associated with crime: one study found that two thirds of the total cost of conduct disorder was related to crime. Large costs were also associated with disruptive education, being in care, and receiving benefits (Scott *et al.* 2001).

It has been noted that it is rare to find an antisocial adult who did not exhibit conduct problems as a child (Robins 1966, 1978), and approximately 40–50 per cent of children with conduct disorder go on to develop antisocial personality disorder as adults (American Academy of Child and Adolescent Psychiatry 1997; Loeber 1982; Rutter and Giller 1983). The Cambridge study in delinquent development found that early starting patterns of conduct disorder were remarkably stable, with half of the most antisocial boys at ages 8 to 10 still being antisocial at age 14 and 43 per cent remaining among the most antisocial at age 18 (Farrington 1989; Farrington, Loeber and Van Kammen 1990).

Other psychiatric disturbances associated with childhood conduct disorder are substance abuse, mania, schizophrenia and obsessive compulsive disorder, major depressive disorders and panic disorder (Maughan and Rutter 1998; Robins 1966). Adult antisocial behaviours associated with childhood conduct disorder include theft, violence towards people and property, drink driving, use of illegal drugs, carrying and using weapons, and group violence (Farrington 1995). Conduct disorder in childhood has also been linked to incomplete schooling, joblessness and consequent financial dependency, poor interpersonal relationships and abuse of the next generation of children (Robins 1991; Rutter and Giller 1983). Problem behaviour that starts in adolescence affects about one quarter of the general population, and generally does not persist into adulthood (Moffitt 2003).

2 Young People With More Than One Disorder (Comorbidity)

Conduct disorder is itself a complex disorder, which is further complicated by the fact that young people with behaviour disorders often have other conditions (Greene *et al.* 2002; Maughan *et al.* 2004). Comorbidity can be defined as the 'simultaneous occurrence of two or more unrelated conditions' (Caron and Rutter 1991, p.1063). Disorders that are likely to occur with conduct disorder are: attention-deficit/hyperactivity disorder (ADHD), oppositional defiant disorder (ODD) and depression (Greene *et al.* 2002; Rey 1994). Comorbidity can have important implications for the development, diagnosis and treatment of conduct disorder (Stahl and Clarizio 1999):

- Comorbidity in teenagers is more common than a single disorder. For this reason it is vital that a comprehensive initial assessment is carried out.

- Issues arise as to the need for a combined category for disorders that commonly occur together. This has been the case for the ICD-10 category of hyperkinetic conduct disorder, which refers to a comorbid conduct disorder and hyperactivity disorder.

- When a disorder typically precedes another such as in the relationship with oppositional defiant and conduct disorder, it has been suggested that the first disorder could be a vulnerability factor for the second. A series of studies on clinic samples showed that among those with conduct disorder, the risk for affective disorder is increased and vice versa (Alessi and Magen 1988; Chiles, Miller and Cox 1980).

- Comorbidity with conduct disorder complicates treatment since it may be difficult to decide what the main focus of the treatment should be.

Conditions and behaviours associated with conduct disorder are listed below.

Oppositional defiant disorder (ODD)

ODD symptoms are sometimes followed by conduct disorder, and thus a large proportion of young people with conduct disorder may simultaneously qualify for a diagnosis of ODD (Faraone *et al*. 1991; Spitzer, Davies and Barclay 1991; Walker *et al*. 1991). Some clinicians have argued that ODD can be a developmental precursor to, and therefore a risk factor for, the development of conduct disorder (Lahey, Loeber and Frick 1992). Reversely, early-onset conduct disorder has been seen as a risk factor for ODD, and comorbid ODD in conduct disordered young people will often result in aggression, and persistent or worsening conduct problems over time (Lahey, Moffitt and Caspi 2003). Greene *et al*. (2002) found that ODD comorbid with conduct disorder was associated with higher rates of depression and bipolar disorder than those diagnosed with ODD alone. However, the relationship between conduct disorder and ODD is still unclear.

Attention-deficit hyperactivity disorder (ADHD)

It may be difficult to distinguish between ADHD and conduct or oppositional behaviour. Some see hyperactivity as virtually a prerequisite for conduct disorder (McArdle, O'Brien and Kolvin 1995), whilst others have suggested that its presence can predict the early onset of conduct disorder (Lahey *et al*. 1995). It has also been suggested that conduct disorder and ADHD have similar causes (Lahey and Waldman 2003), partly explained by genetic influences (Dick *et al*. 2005).

A study of twins has found that all sub-types of ADHD are associated with higher rates of conduct disorder and oppositional defiant disorder (Willcutt *et al*. 1999). The strongest association was found with symptoms of hyperactivity/impulsivity, whilst inattention symptoms were found to be more linked to depression.

Co-occurrence of hyperactivity and conduct problems has been associated with poorer outcomes than either disorder on its own (Lahey and Waldman 2003). One study found that young people with comorbid conduct problems and hyperactivity/impulsivity had a higher risk of being involved in crime than those with a single diagnosis (Babinski, Hartsough and Lambert 1999), although this finding was not supported by another report (MacDonald and Achenbach 1999). This comorbid diagnostic group also seem to have higher occurrences of behavioural problems at school, contact with mental health services, substance abuse and suicidal behaviour (MacDonald and Achenbach 1999).

Depression

Conduct disorder has been associated with depression in several studies (Angold and Costello 1993; Feldman and Wilson 1997; Zoccolillo 1992), and the rates of depression in conduct disordered young people approach 25 per cent in some samples (Steiner and Wilson 1999). Conduct disorder with depression seems to place adolescents at a high risk for future emotional, behavioural, academic, social and vocational problems (Reinecke 1995). Depression has also been found to be prevalent amongst imprisoned young offenders (Hagell 2002; National Statistics 2000).

Suicide

A link between suicidal and antisocial behaviour has been suggested in one review (Fox and Hawton 2004). Adolescents with disruptive disorders have been found to be at risk for suicide when there is comorbid substance abuse and a past history of suicidal behaviour (Renaud et al. 1999). Suicidal thoughts and suicide attempts are known to be high amongst imprisoned young offenders. In one survey 20 per cent of male remand young offenders said they had attempted suicide at some time in their life, 17 per cent in the year before the interview and 3 per cent in the previous week (National Statistics 2000).

Substance abuse

The risk of substance abuse has also been found to be high within the conduct disordered population (Disney et al. 1999; Robins and McEvoy

1990). The presence of conduct disorder has been associated with an early start of substance use, and this use is considered more likely to develop into abuse (Robins and McEvoy 1990).

A distinction can be made between those adolescents who are conduct disordered independent of substance abuse, and those who become conduct disordered when the behaviours warranting diagnosis are related to alcohol or drug involvement. Brown *et al.* (1996) studied a large adolescent population admitted to alcohol and treatment programmes and found that 95 per cent fulfilled DSM-III-R criteria for conduct disorder[1] (Brown *et al.* 1996). These findings were mirrored in a further study of 137 substance-abusing adolescents with conduct disorder. Four years after treatment it was found that 61 per cent of the study group met the DSM-III-R criteria for antisocial personality disorder (Myers, Stewart and Brown 1998).

There is a strong link between substance misuse and offending, and this is also true for young people in the criminal justice system (Hagell 2002). From a sample of 600 young people appearing in court, 15 per cent were judged by their youth justice worker to have a problem with drugs or alcohol. The proportion rose to 37 per cent for those whose offending was classed as serious or persistent (Audit Commission 1996).

Learning disabilities

Rates of learning disabilities have been reported to be high, but variable, amongst young people diagnosed with conduct disorder (BMA Board of Science 2006; Smith 1995; Steiner and Wilson 1999). Early weakness in verbal learning and reasoning has been found to modestly predict later offending, conduct disorder and antisocial outcomes, whilst there appears to be no link between the level of non-verbal intelligence and those outcomes (Nigg and Huang-Pollock 2003). Although a significant proportion of conduct disordered young people have learning disabilities, this review focuses on interventions for those with average IQ (intelligence quotient) test scores of 80 or higher.

Note

1   DSM-III-R were the US diagnostic criteria preceding the current DSM-IV criteria (Appendix 1).

3 Aetiology and Developmental Pathways

Research into the aetiology (or cause) of conduct problems has focused on risk factors that appear to make the onset of conduct disorder more likely. A number of different approaches are discussed in the literature from biological, psychological and sociological perspectives (Lahey *et al.* 2003). Similarly, resilience research has looked at protective factors that work against the presence of risky circumstances.

A definitive model for conduct disorder and its causes has yet to be developed (American Academy of Child and Adolescent Psychiatry 1997) and a number of factors have been identified that are thought to increase the likelihood of developing conduct problems. These can be divided broadly into factors that are relevant to children themselves (biology) and factors associated with the child's environment (family, school). When looking at risk factors, it is important to bear in mind that most of these have little effect when they occur on their own (Fonagy *et al.* 2002; Rutter 1999). Young people in certain situations, such as those being taken into care, are more likely to have been subject to a range of the factors presented here, and the care they subsequently receive may protect, or place them at further risk. Similarly, whilst family risk factors are considered to be substantial, research has also shown that children can have an adverse effect on their parents' behaviour, which again presents a further risk factor for sustained conduct problems (Bell 1968; Rutter 2005).

We currently know much more about risk indicators than we do about risk mechanisms and there is still a way to go before we reach an adequate understanding of risk and protective processes in children's development (Rutter 1999). Most young people who grow up in adversity do well, and the reasons for why some young people develop conduct disorder or become involved in offending are complex.

Individual factors

The development of antisocial behaviour has been divided into two pathways: life-course persistent and adolescent-limited (Moffitt *et al.* 1996). The former begins in childhood and has its origins in neuro-developmental processes. The latter has its origins in social processes and begins in adolescence. Studies have shown that the life-course persistent path of antisocial behaviour is predicted by individual characteristics such as uncontrolled temperament, neurological abnormalities, delayed motor developments, intellectual ability, reading difficulties, hyperactivity, slow heart-rate and poor scores on neuropsychological tests of memory (Moffitt 2003).

Having behaviour problems at pre-school age has been identified as the single best predictor of later antisocial behaviour (White *et al.* 2004). At this early age, behaviour problems are often seen in relation to a child's temperament, activity level, attentiveness, how they adapt to new situations, and levels of distress (Bailey 1997). Individual differences in temperament emerge very early in life. Pre-school children with 'difficult temperament' show high rates of mother–child conflict (Lee and Bates 1985; Thomas, Chess and Birch 1968). Difficult temperament is possibly an inborn dimension but influenced by very early social experiences (Kingston and Prior 1995; Sanson *et al.* 1993).

Attention difficulties have also been linked to conduct disorder, as indicated by the common comorbidity with ADHD. MacDonald and Achenbach (1999) found that the combination of both attention and conduct problems led to more behavioural problems in school, more contact with mental health services, higher levels of substance abuse and increased prevalence of suicidal behaviour, than either problem on its own (MacDonald and Achenbach 1999).

Age and gender have both been found to correlate with antisocial behaviour, but the relationship is complex and confounded by social and genetic variables (Meyer *et al.* 2000; Rutter 2003a). For example, boys have been found to be more vulnerable to adverse parenting environments (Morrell and Murray 2003), and more likely to be diagnosed with conduct disorder and to show aggressive symptoms in early life (Dodge 2003). However, a meta-analysis on this topic found that gender was not a significant influence on antisocial behaviour compared with genetic and social factors (Rhee and Waldman 2003).

There is increasing evidence of genetic influences on antisocial behaviour (Lahey and Waldman 2003; Moffitt 2003; Rhee and Waldman 2003; Tremblay 2003). Investigating genetic influences on conduct disorder is complex, but one suggested model is that a genetic vulnerability for conduct disorder is triggered by environmental risk and further mediated by factors such as poor coping skills (American Academy of Child and Adolescent Psychiatry 1997; Meyer *et al.* 2000; Rutter 2003a).

The development of testosterone levels in individuals has been paralleled to the development of criminal behaviour, but the association is again complex and it has not been linked with aggressive behaviour per se. Some research has suggested a link between high testosterone levels in foetal life and later behaviour. Similarly, high serotonin (5-HT) levels have been associated with impulsivity and aggression (Moffitt 2003).

Cognitive impairment is another risk factor for conduct disorder and offending. In a small sample of 55 young children with conduct disorder, Gilmour *et al.* (2004) found that two thirds had pragmatic language impairments and other behavioural features (independent of IQ scores). These were similar in nature and degree to those of children with autism (Gilmour *et al.* 2004). Damage to the frontal lobe of the brain has been found to impact on a person's behaviour, although the relationship is not clear and study results tend to vary. Some studies have linked impairment in executive function and head injury to antisocial behaviour, but a statistically significant relationship has been disputed by others (Ishikawa and Raine 2003). Again, research tends to conclude that biological and social factors interact in the development of antisocial behaviour (Lahey and Waldman 2003).

Family factors

Parenting and family interaction factors have been found to account for 30–40 per cent of the variation in children's antisocial behaviour (Barlow 1999; Patterson, DeBaryshe and Ramsey 1989; Yoshikawa 1994). Family factors that may influence the development of conduct disorder are the degree of parental involvement, conflict management, and inconsistent or harsh discipline (Brennan, Grekin and Mednick 2003; Burke, Loeber and Birmaher 2003; Patterson *et al.* 1989; Sameroff, Peck and Eccles 2004).

Families of children and adolescents with conduct problems are thought to have greater levels of defensive communications and lower levels of supportive communication compared with families of non-delinquent children (Alexander and Parsons 1973). Mothers who smoke more than half a packet of cigarettes each day during pregnancy are at greater risk of having children with conduct problems than those who do not smoke during pregnancy (Wakschlag *et al.* 1997). Poverty and low socio-economic status have also been associated with conduct problems, although there is still debate as to how these effects are mediated (Petras *et al.* 2004; Spender and Scott 1996). Poverty has been found to impact negatively on parenting (Rutter 1999).

A large meta-analysis has looked at various family factors that correlate with conduct problems (Loeber and Stouthamer-Loeber 1986). Four paradigms of family influence (parenting) were identified.

1. *Neglect paradigm*: parents may spend insufficient time engaging in positive interactions with their children. They may be unaware of their children's behaviour, ignore behaviour problems, or be unaware of their children's whereabouts. The lack of involvement may contribute to the child's withdrawal from their parents. It seems that a lack of the father's involvement is more strongly related to delinquency and aggression than a lack of involvement of the mother. Although some studies have found that employed mothers tend to have more delinquent children than those not in employment, this relationship disappears when socio-economic status or parent and child characteristics are accounted for (Robins 1966; Wadsworth 1979). Lack of child supervision has also been significantly related to delinquency.

2. *Conflict paradigm*: conflict escalations between parents and their children are part of the family pattern. The conflict may be a result of the young person's disobedience but the parent may be unable to adequately curtail this. In particular, the meta-analysis found significant associations between a lack of consistency and strictness of discipline and conduct problems. There was also a significant relationship between perceived unfairness of punishment and delinquency.

3. *Deviant behaviours/attitudes paradigm:* parental deviance or lawbreaking may encourage children to imitate parental deviant behaviours. A significant relationship has been found between parental criminal activity or aggression and later delinquency and conduct problems. Deviant behaviours in parents, such as dishonesty, tolerance of children's delinquency and encouragement of aggression, was manifested in the children's delinquency or aggressive behaviour.

4. *Disruption paradigm:* unusual events, such as the break-up of a marriage, will disrupt normal family behaviour patterns. This may lead parents to display irritable and aggressive behaviours to which children may respond in a similar manner or simply avoid the parents. Marital conflict was found to be a statistically significant predictor of children's delinquent or antisocial behaviour, and a more important influence than parental absence. Mothers' physical illness was a predictor of later delinquency, whilst the same relationship was not seen in terms of fathers' health. One study found a strong relationship between mothers' depression and later antisocial behaviour (Richman, Stevenson and Graham 1982).

School factors

The main purpose of schools is to educate, and part of this is the important role they play in the socialisation of children. It has been argued that whilst the family is the most important influence on child behaviour in the early years of development, children's self-regulatory capacities are further elaborated in settings such as school and the peer group (Rutter 1996; Snyder, Reid and Patterson 2003). Whilst the school may not be a risk factor for conduct disorder in itself, there are factors within the school environment that may facilitate further developments towards antisocial behaviour in certain children (Gottfredson, Wilson and Skroban Najaka 2002). For example, the school playground can be an arena for early deviant behaviour. Snyder *et al.* (2003) found only 1.7 per cent of children's aversive behaviour and 3 per cent of their physical aggression towards other children resulted in adult intervention.

The quality of schools has also been linked to conduct disorder in young people (Gottfredson *et al.* 2002; Kazdin 1995; Rutter 1999). Antisocial children are much less likely to get encouragement from teachers for appropriate behaviour and more likely to get punished for negative conduct than well-behaved children. Schools that categorise pupils as deviant and failures, ignore repeated truancy and suspend or expel the most difficult students contribute to the development of violent behaviour (Marshall and Watt 1999).

School is also an arena for establishing friendships. Deviant peer behaviour has been found to be a risk factor for the development of aggression in young people (Sameroff et al. 2004; Schaeffer et al. 2003). Early peer rejection has been linked to conduct disorder in some studies (Miller-Johnson et al. 2002) but not in others (Schaeffer et al. 2003). Aggression has also been linked to bullying behaviour, or being bullied. One study found that bullies and victims were similar in reactive aggression, but that proactive aggression was found in bullies only (Camodeca and Goossens 2005). Being a bully has been associated with delinquent behaviour (van der Wal, de Wit and Hirasing 2003).

Conversely, schools that target violent or bullying behaviour, encourage school staff to build warm and close relationships with pupils, and teach social as well as academic skills, have been found to reduce problem behaviour (Battistich et al. 1996; Gottfredson et al. 2002; Mytton et al. 2006; Olweus 1994; Smith, Ananiadou and Cowie 2003).

Protective factors

Many young people will avoid being diagnosed with conduct disorder or becoming involved in offending despite having many of the risk factors described above – they are, in current jargon, 'resilient'. Resilience is the ability to resist negative influences in spite of growing up in adverse circumstances. Little is known about the exact nature of the development of resilience, but one identified factor is the genetic effect on an individual's vulnerability to stress factors in their social environment (Brooks 1994; Rutter 2003b). When some of the risk factors identified above are reversed, they present as protective factors. For example, *low* level of parental physical punishment of young offenders has been associated with lowering the risk that the offending behaviour persists into adulthood (Stouthamer-Loeber et al. 2004). Late resilience, emerging in the transition to adulthood, has been identified as a recovery factor in some individuals (Masten et al. 2004).

Self-esteem is a key variable in developing resilience. Children who are resilient are able to adapt and grow using coping strategies (such as

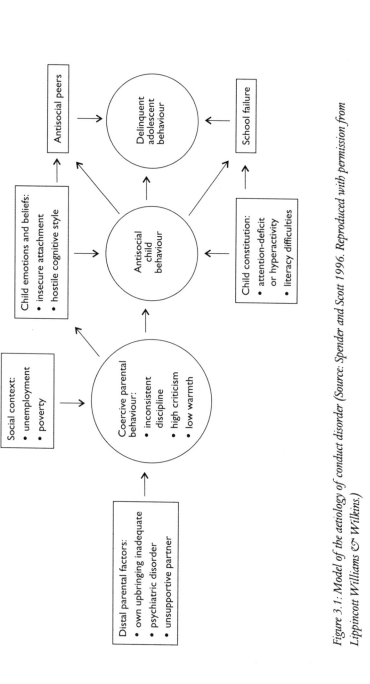

Figure 3.1: Model of the aetiology of conduct disorder (Source: Spender and Scott 1996. Reproduced with permission from Lippincott Williams & Wilkins.)

knowing when to ask for help), possess a sense of personal control over their lives, and are able to learn from mistakes rather than feeling helpless. Resilient children have often been found to draw on support from adults outside their immediate family, such as teachers, neighbours or relatives (Werner and Smith 1982). Resilience in young people is best fostered by a warm, affectionate, and emotionally supportive environment which has a relatively stable structure and clear boundaries.

The social environment is also an important factor in developing resilience in young people. One study looking at boys in a high-risk group found that those living in neighbourhoods with low levels of deviant behaviour were less likely to become involved in criminal activity (Petras *et al.* 2004). The same study also found that a high level of parental monitoring significantly reduced the risk of arrest in children in spite of increasing aggression.

Knowing about the development of resilience in children and young people can help us design effective interventions to promote this development. The most promising interventions for treating conduct disorder or reducing offending tend to work with young people to help them realise their potential instead of engaging in activities that are destructive both to themselves and their environment (see Figure 3.1).

4 Prevention

Conduct disorder in adolescence is difficult to treat (Bailey 1996; Frick 2001), and the most promising research evidence available is concerned with how the disorder can be prevented by interventions in childhood, particularly by using parenting programmes (Kellermann 1998; Reid, Webster-Stratton and Baydar 2004).

The most critical factors identified as being central to treatment efficacy for conduct disorder are 1. age at which the intervention is introduced and 2. clinical course and severity of the disorder (Moretti *et al.* 1997). As children move outside their families, other influences, such as peer relationships and school functioning, become more salient to the development and maintenance of conduct problems. This raises conceptual issues about the type and duration of treatments, and which treatments will be effective for young people at different developmental stages and with different types of conduct disorder.

For example, support for parents of children aged 0–3 has been shown to impact on behaviour in the long term. One randomised controlled trial carried out in the UK looked at the impact of social support in pregnancy on a range of child and mother outcomes. During this trial mothers with a history of low-birthweight babies were provided with a 24-hour contact number and home visits by a midwife. During the home visits midwives would discuss issues of concern to the mothers, and provide practical information and advice. When appropriate they would make referrals to other agencies. Evidence of benefit from the programme persisted at six weeks and one year after birth. Babies in the intervention group had higher birthweight and mothers' health was better than in the control group

(Oakley, Rajan and Grant 1990). At seven-year follow-up the differences in outcomes remained, and behaviour problems were more frequent in children in the control group (Oakley *et al.* 1996).

Evidence from the US has also found that long-term home-visiting for disadvantaged families, from pregnancy and onwards (1–5 years), impacts positively on later behaviour (McCord, Spatz Widom and Crowell 2001). One study followed up the children after 15 years and found that children in the treatment group (who received regular nurse visits from prenatal to two years of age) had fewer arrests, convictions, probation violations and incidents of running away (Olds *et al.* 1998).

The UK Sure Start initiative was based on a trial from the US. This showed that social support during the first three years of a child's life impacted on social outcomes in adolescence, including antisocial behaviour and self-reported involvement in crime (Schweinhart and Weikart 1980). These effects were sustained in adulthood, which also made this a cost-effective intervention. The main savings from the programme were mainly related to reduced crime by males in the intervention group, compared with those in the control group (Belfield *et al.* 2006; Moffitt *et al.* 1996; Rutter, Giller and Hagell 1998). Behaviour problems that persist from early childhood have been found to have a stronger negative impact than problem behaviours that start in adolescence (Moffitt 2003; Rutter *et al.* 1998). Intervening in pre-adolescence may therefore help prevent conduct disorder at a later stage. In 2006 the National Institute for Health and Clinical Excellence (NICE) in collaboration with the Social Care Institute for Excellence (SCIE) made recommendations to the National Health Service (NHS) in England and Wales that parent training/education programmes should be available for the management of conduct disorders in children aged 12 years or younger. The guidance recommends group-based programmes, but specifies that individual programmes may be required for families with complex needs. A further specification is that the chosen model of parenting programme should be evidence-based (National Institute for Health and Clinical Excellence 2006). The long-term effect of parent training programmes has not yet been established.

A Cochrane review has looked at the effect of media-based parenting programmes. These are delivered to parents via a videotape, the internet, a manual, or as a combination of these, with minimal input from professionals. Only programmes based on behavioural or cognitive behavioural therapy were included. Nine studies were found that looked at such programmes' effect on conduct problems. Although not as effective as therapist-led programmes, media-based parenting courses yielded statistically significant improvements over waiting-list controls. The authors suggest that such programmes could be used in a step-based approach to care, to free up therapist time for those families that need more intense intervention. The studies in this systematic review included children aged 2–15, but the majority were under ten years of age (Montgomery 2005).

Linking the interest of families and teachers (LIFT) is a programme developed by Oregon Social Learning Center. The intervention consists of three main components: parent management training, social and problem-solving skills training for pupils, and behaviour management during breaks/play time. A cluster-randomised trial looked at the effect of this intervention when delivered to pupils at age ten (grade 5 in the US), on their subsequent arrest rates and substance use at age 13 (grade 8 in the US). Two and a half years after the end of the intervention, 10.3 per cent of the comparison group had been arrested at least once, compared with 4.1 per cent of the intervention group. No significant differences were found in relation to tobacco and marijuana use (Eddy et al. 2003). Missing data was a problem in this study, which weakens the results.

For older children, screening for violent behaviour in primary care could be one way of preventing problem behaviour escalating into full-blown conduct disorder. In one randomised controlled trial from the US, children aged 7–15 who attended an outpatient paediatric clinic were screened for psychosocial problems using the Pediatric Symptom Checklist (PSC-17). Parents were sent videotapes and a manual, and supported by a parent educator once a week, over the telephone. The whole intervention lasted 13 weeks and included role-play and discussion topics. Take-up amongst parents was relatively low: 53 per cent completed at least one educational telephone session. The intervention appeared to reduce parental depression and use of corporal punishment. It also reduced aggressive and delinquent behaviour, when measured on parent report, but not according to children's own reports (Wagman Borowsky et al. 2004).

For looked after children and young people, a history of placement disruption tends to correlate with complex mental health needs. Instability in placement appears to be enhanced by disruptive behaviour; however, the relationship is not clear. It may also be that frequent moves contribute to the development of problem behaviour (Stanley, Riordan and Alaszewski 2005). Conduct disorder in looked after children and young people may be prevented by securing stable placements, and early attention to their mental health needs.

5 Measuring and Assessing Problem Behaviour

According to the American Academy of Child and Adolescent Psychiatry (1997), assessment requires the collection of data from a number of informants in multiple settings using multiple methods. The assessment process is important and other conditions (such as hyperkinetic disorder) need to be established before a diagnosis of conduct disorder or oppositional defiant disorder is made. The *International Classification of Diseases* (ICD-10) was developed by the World Health Organization (1994) and approved by member countries. This includes diagnostic criteria for conduct disorder, as outlined in Appendix 1. Also commonly referred to is the *Diagnostic and Statistical Manual of Mental Disorders* (DSM-IV), developed by the American Psychiatric Association (1994). Their diagnostic criteria for conduct disorder are also outlined in Appendix 1.

A number of tools can be used to assess young people with behaviour problems. These tools allocate scores to each answer provided by the respondent (parent, teacher, child). The scores are interpreted within a diagnostic framework corresponding to ICD-10 or DSM-IV. Diagnostic tools are assessed according to their reliability and validity. Reliability refers to whether the tool consistently produces the same results over time and across populations. Validity refers to a tool's sensitivity (correct identification of cases) and specificity (correct identification of non-cases). Two of the most commonly used tools are the Child Behavior Checklist (Achenbach and Edelbrock 1991) and Goodman's Strengths and Difficulties Questionnaire (Goodman 1997), which are briefly described below.

The Child Behavior Checklist (CBCL) is part of the Achenbach System of Empirically Based Assessment. It is one of the most commonly used measures both in research and practice, and assesses competencies and problems. The CBCL is developed for ages 6–18 (a separate tool is available for younger children) and is designed for parents or the extended family. The tool takes 15 minutes to fill in and provides an in-depth assessment (120 items) across a range of scales including aggressive, delinquent and externalising behaviour, and attention problems. It should only be administered by those with psychological training. The CBCL is complemented by other assessment tools in the Achenbach System, such as the Teacher's Report Form, Youth Self-Report Form, and forms for doing observation and semi-structured interviews. For more information see www.aseba.org.

The CBCL has been validated and adapted to different cultures (Drotar, Stein and Perrin 1995; Lowe 1998). Literature reviews looking at the reliability and validity of the CBCL have found that the scale is highly sensitive to the presence of conduct disorder, but that its specificity (detection of non-cases) is relatively low (Lowe 1998). One review concludes that the tool is effective in screening for conduct disorder, but that a clinical diagnosis should not be based solely on the CBCL (Lowe 1998).

Goodman's Strengths and Difficulties Questionnaire (SDQ) has not been around as long as the CBCL, but is widely used. It is developed for 4–16-year-olds and designed for report by children and young people themselves, parents and teachers. It takes five minutes to fill in the questionnaire, which consists of five scales, each of which has five sub-questions (25 items in all). The five sub-scales are: emotional symptoms; conduct problems; hyperactivity; peer problems; prosocial (strengths). No specialist training is required to administer this tool, which may explain why it has gained such popularity over a relatively short time span. A special version has been developed for use in follow-up assessment. All tools are available for free and in different languages from www.sdqinfo.com. The SDQ has not been subject to the same amount of external scrutiny as the CBCL, which is probably due to it being a relatively recent development.

For young offenders, the Youth Justice Board has developed Asset, which is a tool to assess factors contributing to a young person's offending. The tool is used by all youth offending teams (YOTs) in England and Wales, for every young person who comes into contact with the criminal justice system. Asset is a comprehensive tool which looks at all aspects of a young person's life, including family relationships, education, substance use, mental health, and behaviour. The assessment includes a section looking specifically at the views of the young person (Youth Justice Board 2006). For more information see: www.yjb.gov.uk/en-gb/practitioners/ Assessment.

Although assessment is central to the work of both researchers and practitioners, one study has reported that young people find some psychometric tests to be boring and difficult to fill in (Feilzer *et al.* 2004).

There are many other scales for measuring children's behaviour, social competencies, aggression and delinquent behaviour. There are also scales developed to measure parents' stress levels and family functioning. Alongside the reorganisation of children's services in the UK, the Department for Education and Skills has developed a common assessment framework for all agencies working with children. It builds upon previous developments, such as the Looking After Children materials (1995) and the Assessment Framework (2000), and offers a single approach to undertaking the key processes of assessment, planning, intervention and review based on an understanding of children's developmental needs, and their parents' capacities to respond to these needs in the context of their families and communities (Department for Education and Skills 2006b).

The common assessment framework is developed to help practitioners work preventively, and identify children at risk rather than those who are in need of immediate protection. The framework is a non-statutory guidance, and is not intended to replace assessment tools already used by specialist agencies, but as an additional resource. For example, the youth justice services will continue to use their tailor-made assessment tools for young offenders, but these may be informed by the common assessment framework. It may be of particular use for when a young person's needs fall outside of the specialist agencies, which is likely to be the case both for young offenders and those young people that are diagnosed with conduct disorder.

Measures used in the included studies

Tools to measure problem behaviour are essential when researching interventions, but one problem when reviewing the literature is the wide range of tools that are used. For example, some of the scales used by studies in this review include: the Child Behavior Checklist (used by Ercan *et al.* 2003; Gundersen and Svartdal 2006; Ogden and Halliday-Boykins 2004; Santisteban *et al.* 2003; Schoenwald, Halliday-Boykins and Henggeler 2003); the Weinberger Adjustment Inventory (used by Steiner, Saxena and

Chang 2003); the Nisonger Child Behaviour Rating Form (used by Reyes *et al.* 2006); the Child and Adolescent Disruptive Behaviour Inventory (used by Gundersen and Svartdal 2006); the Social Skills Rating System (used by Gundersen and Svartdal 2006; Ogden and Halliday-Boykins 2004); the School Adjustment Index (used by Arbuthnot and Gordon 1986); the Self-Control Rating Scale (used by Etscheid 1991); the Disability Assessment Schedule (used by Hill-Tout, Pithouse and Lowe 2003); the Adolescents' Risky-Behavior Scale (used by Nickel *et al.* 2004); the State-Trait Anger Expression Inventory (used by Nickel *et al.* 2004); and the Self-Report Delinquency Scale (used by Ogden and Halliday-Boykins 2004).

Some of these tools were developed by the researchers carrying out the study. Others, such as the Child Behavior Checklist, have been tested for validity across populations and in different countries. When reading research it is important to pay attention to the tools used to measure behaviour before and after an intervention. For example, some tools may measure aggressive intent instead of actual aggressive behaviour. It is also important to note the difference between measures by self-report, observation, and administrative records such as court appearances or truancy rates. Police records are likely to report lower levels of offending because much offending is not detected by the police. As in practice assessment, use of more than one source of information is likely to strengthen the results of a study.

6 Services for Adolescents

> ...children and young people with mental health problems is not just the responsibility of specialist CAMHS. In many cases, the intervention that makes a difference will come from another service. For example, a child presenting with behavioural problems may make better progress if his/her literacy problems are also addressed, in which case an input is required from education. The lack of provision in one service may impact on the ability of other services to be effective. (Department of Health 2004, p.7)

At present there is a lack of appropriate services for conduct disordered adolescents, and in particular the older age group of 16- and 17-year-olds. This is also true for other mental health problems (BMA Board of Science 2006; Kerfoot, Panayiotopoulos and Harrington 2004). Nevertheless, the number of young offenders under the care of CAMHS increased between 2003 and 2005. This is reflected in a rise in targeted CAMHS services for young offenders by approximately 9 per cent in the same period, including both specialist teams and CAMHS workers in non-CAMHS teams (Barnes *et al.* 2005).

Inter-agency collaboration in relation to conduct disorder and youth offending has been recognised as being difficult, with young people falling between agencies due to the complexity of their situation (Feilzer *et al.* 2004; Kelly *et al.* 2003; Salmon and Rapport 2005). Young people with conduct disorder have also been found to be harder to engage in clinical work (Barber, Tischler and Healy 2006; Baruch, Gerber and Fearon 1998). A small survey of children and young people using CAMHS found that those with conduct problems were less likely to be satisfied with the service they received (Barber *et al.* 2006).

However, a collaborative approach across services is essential for young people with conduct disorder as no agency is likely to be able to successfully deal with this client group on their own (Salmon and Rapport 2005). A joined-up approach also has the benefit of making services more accessible to young people and their families (Kelly *et al.* 2003; Percy-Smith 2005). A UK survey found that links between social services departments and CAHMS were particularly good in relation to multidisciplinary assessment and treatment delivery (Kerfoot *et al.* 2004). The main disadvantage of CAMHS was seen as being long waiting lists and inaccessible service, something that has also been highlighted by other studies (BMA Board of Science 2006; Potter, Langley and Sakhuja 2005).

The reorganisation of children's services, under the agenda of Every Child Matters: Change for Children, offers an opportunity to set up systems to improve collaboration for conduct disordered young people and young offenders. By 2006 local plans for children and young people form a basis for a partnership approach to commissioning and delivering services. By 2008 all areas should have established children's trusts and arrangements should be in place to support integrated working at all levels. Included in this joint approach is the common assessment framework, which is a standardised approach to assess a child's needs and strengths, taking account of the role of parents, carers and environmental factors on their development (Department for Education and Skills 2006b). The integrated children's system (ICS) is another initiative to enhance information sharing across agencies. This is for all managers and practitioners who work with children in need, and all authorities should have a fully operational system in place by January 2007 (Department for Education and Skills 2006c).

Primary care trusts and strategic health authorities are key partners in developing children's trusts, and the new framework encompasses collaboration between schools, social services and youth offending services. The joint inspection framework for children's services will have a role in assessing the extent to which these policies are successfully implemented and maintained (Percy-Smith 2005).

Child protection falls outside of the boundaries of the children's trusts. In the new framework the Area Child Protection Committees are replaced by Safeguarding Children Boards, with representatives from all relevant agencies. In child protection as in all services for children, local authorities have been charged with ensuring that services are joined up across agencies.

Every Child Matters also states that protocols for links to acute trusts should be in place. The establishment of these will be particularly important for a small group of young people, when their conduct disorders have escalated to the extent that they require emergency psychiatric care and admission to a psychiatric inpatient unit with specialist resources. Links between tier 4 and community services can be strengthened in multi-agency collaboration. An example of this is the Behaviour Resource Service in Southampton, a joint initiative with social services, CAMHS and education. The service offers short-term residential assessment and treatment for young people, alongside a multiprofessional community team comprising: one team manager, one family therapist, one social worker, one teacher, two community support workers, one nurse therapist, two part-time educational psychologists, and one day per week input from a community paediatrician (Kelly *et al.* 2003).

Some studies have found that the awareness of mental health problems in children is poor amongst tier 1 professions such as general practitioners (GPs) (Foreman 2001), school nurses (Richardson and Partridge 2000) and teachers (Ford and Nikapota 2000), and that referrers are sometimes unfamiliar with the structure of CAMHS and services available. This is likely to vary between areas. Referrers, on the other hand, have emphasised the need for quick and easy access and improved communication (Potter *et al.* 2005). It may be that the new framework for children's services will offer CAMHS teams the opportunity to strengthen their role as consultants to carers, social workers and schools (Stanley *et al.* 2005).

The Youth Justice Board has set up its own national standards. Under these, the Chief Officers' Steering Group:

> must ensure that the work of the YOTs and the Youth Justice Plan is consistent with, and linked to, other relevant local plans including: Crime and Disorder Strategy; Children's Services Plan; Health Improvement Plan (the NHS plan in Wales); local Drug Action Teams Plan (young person's substance misuse plan); the strategy for the local Connexions Service (Extending Entitlement in Wales); Education Development plan; Behaviour Support Plan; and other plans in relation to young people. (Youth Justice Board 2004, pp.6–7)

The Youth Justice Board has produced a series of guidelines called *Key Elements of Effective Practice*. These describe features of effective youth justice services and cover a range of areas including parenting, assessment and offending behaviour. The series' mental health manual provides a guideline in terms of assessment, training, management, service development, monitoring and evaluation. It emphasises collaboration between youth offending teams, CAMHS and other agencies. Central to service delivery is assessment, which informs individual mental health intervention plans for young offenders. It states that:

> Where ever possible, the practitioner should take into account the young person's wider needs alongside their mental health needs. These would include housing, social and family care. Due consideration should also be given to their culture and ethnicity. (Youth Justice Board 2003, p.13)

Schools are a logical point of intervention for child mental health services. One survey has found that teachers value support and collaboration with specialist teams (Ford and Nikapota 2000). An example of CAMHS linking in with schools is provided by Richardson and Partridge (2000), whereby monthly consultation meetings were held with CAMHS team members and school nurses. 'School nurses can lack confidence in these areas of work as they and their professional supervisors have little or no mental health training' (p.462). Meetings were used to inform nurses of the local CAMHS structure and functions (including clarifying referral routes), and discussing issues such as bullying, liaising with parents, and managing anxiety within themselves and the school (Richardson and Partridge 2000).

Considering the high prevalence of conduct disorder in looked after children (Green et al. 2005; Kelly et al. 2003), commissioners of services need to pay particular attention to this group. Training of social workers, and ensuring links with CAMHS and child protection social work, is important (Stanley et al. 2005).

The Care Matters green paper highlights functional family therapy as a promising intervention and proposes an evaluation of this approach. Another proposal of the green paper is to create a national centre for excellence in children and family services, which would gather and review emerging evidence, maintain a database of effective practice, and commission new research (Department for Education and Skills 2006a).

Part Two

The Research Base – Techniques for Treating Conduct Disorder and Treatment Approaches for Young Offenders

The research studies that we refer to here were identified in a structured and systematic search for literature. Details of the search are outlined in Appendix 3. Studies and reviews reporting the effectiveness of interventions have been critically appraised according to pre-set criteria, as specified in Appendix 4. The critical appraisals of individual studies and reviews are available on the website of the Royal College of Psychiatry on www.rcpsych.ac.uk/crtu/focus/focuspublications.aspx. Specialist terms are explained not in the text but in the glossary in Appendix 2.

Quality of Research Evidence

There is a large amount of research in this area. Here, we report only on findings from systematic reviews, meta-analyses and controlled trials. This is because our main focus has been on the effectiveness of interventions. A more comprehensive review would also look at qualitative research, to identify service satisfaction, experiences of interventions, and mechanisms underlying the effects found in trials. It can sometimes be difficult to assess whether the young people included in a trial had mild behaviour problems, or a conduct disorder diagnosis. We have only included those studies that state conduct disorder or criminal involvement as a criterion for inclusion. Where a systematic review of an intervention has been carried out, we have only critically appraised and included trials published after this review.

Much of the research carried out is of high quality, but there is a problem with some of the reporting. Key information to look for when assessing the findings of a trial or a systematic review is whether effort has been made to reduce bias. The findings from a trial are less biased if, for example, the researchers used random allocation to treatment groups, standardised pre and post measures, and all subjects were accounted for and included in the final analysis. Bias in a systematic review can be reduced by carrying out a comprehensive search and only including studies which meet specified quality standards. These are standards that we have applied in this review. Appendix 2 provides an overview of key terms used in systematic reviewing and critical appraisal.

Some reviews included here are referred to as being from the Cochrane and Campbell Collaborations. These are organisations dedicated to producing high-quality systematic reviews to support clinical treatment, social interventions and policy decisions. The Cochrane Collaboration focuses on interventions to improve health, and its sister organisation (the Campbell Collaboration) focuses on interventions in education, criminal justice and social welfare.

Some individual studies and reviews report the preciseness of the treatment effect, displayed as a confidence interval or standard deviation. These are calculated statistically, but a crude explanation is that they indicate how the effect would be distributed if a whole population was treated rather than just a sample. A narrow confidence interval, or a small standard deviation, is more precise than a wide confidence interval or a large standard deviation. In meta-analyses, tests are carried out to measure whether the treatment effect is consistent across the included studies. This is called a test for heterogeneity. Although some variability in results is expected by chance, it may not be reasonable to pool findings if the results vary considerably due to differences in participants, clinical setting or treatment protocols (Deeks, Altman and Bradburn 2001).

Not all the interventions presented here were found to be effective. Some were found to make no difference when compared with other treatment approaches or no treatment, and some were found to make problems worse. An important message to bear in mind when looking at the research evidence is that absence of research on a particular intervention is not the same as evidence of no effect. Much of the practice carried out in the UK will not have been subject to a rigorous trial, and this review highlights the lack of UK-based effectiveness research in this field.

Techniques for treating conduct disorder and interventions for young offenders

Presented here are interventions which aim to change the behaviour of the young people, measured by standardised assessment tools. Treatments for conduct disorder are presented under seven chapter headings: individual programmes, family and parenting interventions, school-based interventions, pharmacology, interventions for young people involved in firesetting and arson, and other treatments. Research on interventions for young offenders is presented in Chapter 13.

7 Individual Programmes

Cognitive behaviour therapy

Cognitive behaviour therapy (CBT) is a collective term for programmes that place an emphasis on techniques designed to produce changes in thinking in order to change behaviour or mood (Harrington 2000). The main focus is on learning processes and the ways in which a child's external environment can change both their cognition and behaviour. Training often comprises three stages: identification of a problem, identification of solutions, and practising responses (Beck and Fernandez 1998).

CBT for children and adolescents usually includes a range of behaviour performance-based procedures, and often involves the family or school in therapy. It may include individual work, group sessions or both. The length of treatment varies considerably and depends on the severity of difficulties experienced. Individual programmes for children and adolescents with conduct disorder may take up to 25 or 30 weekly sessions. The therapist is active and involved and attempts to develop a collaborative relationship that stimulates the child to think for him or herself. The approach aims to give the child the opportunity to try things out and develop new skills.

This section reviews the effectiveness of individual CBT programmes delivered to young people in groups or on an individual basis. In practice, CBT approaches are often used in combination with other treatments such as parenting programmes, family therapy or psychotherapy.

One systematic review of CBT interventions found that these programmes were overall effective in reducing anger in children and young people with behaviour problems (Sukhodolsky, Kassinove and Gorman 2004). The programmes included in this review were:

1. skills programmes – use of modelling and behaviour practices

2. affective education – teaching techniques of emotion identification, self-monitoring and relaxation

3. problem-solving programmes – teaching techniques such as self-instruction, consequential thinking and attributional training (training people in making the link between their own effort/behaviour and subsequent successful/failed outcomes).

A fourth type of programme combined different approaches.

The review found an overall effect from such programmes across all outcomes (physical aggression, anger experience, self-control, problem solving, and social skills). The highest effect was found for skills training, followed by multimodal interventions and problem solving. Affective education yielded an overall modest positive effect. Although the review found positive effects from CBT programmes, it is worth noting that of their total sample across all studies (n = 40), only 20 per cent were categorised as having severe problem behaviours. Forty-one per cent had moderate and 39 per cent had mild behaviour problems. The included studies were published between 1974 and 1997.

Another systematic review also found an overall positive, but more modest, effect from CBT programmes on children's behaviour, when combining the effects on antisocial behaviour, social skills and social cognitive skills. When looking at the effect on antisocial behaviour on its own, the effect was much smaller and particularly in relation to administrative outcome measures such as police records and school referrals. This review used similar inclusion criteria for studies as the one by Sukhodolsky *et al.* described above, but including more recent studies (up to year 2000), which may explain the difference in overall treatment effect (Lösel and Beelmann 2003).

The following interventions are at least partly based on cognitive behaviour therapy, although they may emphasise different aspects of the approach. Because interventions generally have the same theoretical underpinnings, differences between programmes are often subtle. Some programmes may focus more on changing behaviour, whilst others have cognitive change as their main target. Few programmes focus exclusively on one or the other. A particular problem in evaluating cognitive behavioural programmes arises from the absence of consensus over what this approach actually encompasses (Feilzer *et al.* 2004).

Motivational interviewing

Originating in substance abuse treatment, motivational interviewing is used to assess service users' attitudes to treatment and motivate them to change their behaviour. It is designed to help them identify behaviours and risk factors that act as barriers to change.

Although behaviour change is central to motivational interviewing, the therapist encourages this indirectly. It is dominated by a 'language of change' and 'reflective listening'. Four basic principles underpin the technique:

1. expressing empathy, through reflective listening

2. highlighting differences between a patient's current situations and aims

3. encouraging patients' own initiative to change

4. 'rolling with resistance' by not actively opposing resistance to change, but encouraging patient confidence to act on self-identified solutions.

Therapists will provide empathy, advice about specific behaviour changes, and practical help such as service referrals. Patients will be made aware that they do have a choice in whether to change or not, but the therapist will emphasise benefits of behaviour change (Bundy 2004; Burke, Arkowitz and Menchola 2003; Miller and Rollnick 2002).

Our searches did not identify any studies on the efficacy of using motivational interviewing with young people or families in relation to conduct disorder or offending, but aspects of this technique are used in multisystemic therapy and in cognitive behaviour therapy (Feilzer et al. 2004). It has been suggested that with young people, attrition is enhanced when the therapist focuses on helping patients to 'understand the nature of the therapeutic setting and to develop certain cognitive capacities for recognising and identifying the meaning of their feelings and how their feelings relate to their actions' (Baruch et al. 1998, p.242). Motivational interviewing may be one tool which can help therapists establish such an understanding of the treatment.

Self-statement modification (SSM)

Self-statement modification is based on the notion that thought processes, even though covert, obey the same laws of learning as overt behaviours. In normal childhood development, self-statements become internalised and form the basis of self-control and self-regulation. The theoretical underpinnings of SSM are that childhood behaviour disorders result from maladaptive internalisation of regulatory self-statements (Dush, Hirt and Schroeder 1989).

SSM combines techniques such as modelling and cognitive-behavioural rehearsal. The main focus of the therapy is self-instruction during tasks to improve their attention and problem solving. These include questions to help clarify the task, provision of answers to the questions and rehearsal to assist planning and also self-guidance instructions on how things should be done. The therapist guides the children through a process where instructions are first said out loud, and gradually reduced to whisper, lip movements, and completely internalised. Self-reinforcing statements are also encouraged. Treatment sessions may last between 15 minutes and one hour.

In a meta-analysis by Dush *et al.* (1989) of self-statement modification in the treatment of child behaviour disorders, 48 per cent of the studies included in the meta-analysis referred to young people under the age of 18 with disruptive/aggressive behaviour or delinquency. Statistically significant findings are not reported, but the effect was found to be larger in delinquent young people than those referred for disruptive/aggressive behaviour. Stronger effects were associated with the use of highly educated therapists, and treatment delivered over several sessions, equalling five to eight hours in total.

SSM is mostly used as one component of a treatment package which includes other training techniques, such as behaviour training, role-play, and token reinforcements, which are described next.

Cognitive skills training/problem-solving skills training

Individuals with conduct disorder have been found to show deficiencies or distortions in cognitive processing. These include generating alternative solutions to interpersonal problems, understanding the consequences of actions, understanding how others feel, and identifying the means to obtain a particular objective (Kazdin 2001).

Common characteristics of problem-solving skills training include:

- emphasis on how young people handle situations – thought processes that are used to aid their responses to interpersonal situations, similar to self-statement modifications described above

- reinforcement and modelling of prosocial behaviours

- structured tasks which are increasingly applied to real-life situations

- active involvement by the therapist by providing cues, feedback and assistance in the development of cognitive skills

- a combination of different techniques used to increase the young person's repertoires of responses to situations.

A well-conducted systematic review of treatments for children and adolescents concluded that training in social problem solving appears effective in reducing aggressive behaviour in the short term, but long-term effects of the treatment are limited (Fonagy *et al.* 2002). Another review (Weisz, Hawley and Doss 2004) identified three trials supporting the effectiveness of one specific type of individual problem-solving skills training developed by Kazdin (Kazdin and Weisz 2003). This training consists of about 20 individual sessions lasting 45 minutes each. The programme teaches five problem-solving steps:

1. identifying the problem

2. linking possible solutions to the problem

3. examining the pros and cons of identified solutions

4. selecting the chosen solution

5. evaluating the choice.

This process is established in the children first during simple games and later by role-playing real problems experienced in the past.

A recent randomised controlled trial conducted in the Netherlands compared two group treatments – a social cognitive intervention programme and a social skills training programme – and a small waiting list control group. The children were aged 9–13 (mean age 11.2), and all met the DSM-IV criteria for conduct disorder (APA 1994), oppositional defiant disorder or disruptive behaviour disorder – not otherwise specific

(DBD-NOS). The treatment was delivered to four children at the time. The social cognitive programme consisted of four components: social information-tion processing, problem-solving abilities, social cognitive skills, and self-control skills. Reflection, homework, prompts, cognitive modelling, role-play, time-out procedure and video feedback were used as tools to teach these components. The training programme taught children social skills and the children earned tokens depending on their behaviour in the sessions (van Manen, Prins and Emmelkamp 2004). Both intervention groups improved significantly over the waiting list control at post-test, but the waiting list control group was very small (n = 15). The social cognitive intervention programme improved children's behaviour significantly more than the social skills training programme, and some of the measures were sustained at follow-up.

Social skills training

Social skills can be defined as a set of competencies that allow young people to initiate and maintain positive social relationships with other people. Social relationships include peer relations, school adjustment and relationships in the larger social environment. Inherent in the definition of conduct disorder are deficits in social functioning. The primary aim of social skills training is to help young people gain acceptance and avoid rejection by others by teaching them how to identify alternative prosocial behaviours/strategies, modelling and simulation of these behaviours, and reinforcement of appropriate behaviours. Teaching young people to monitor, evaluate and reinforce the prosocial skills themselves is an important compo-nent of the training (Kavale et al. 1997).

A meta-analysis of social skills training programmes found that teachers perceived the training to have great benefits, whereas parents believed it to be of limited use (Kavale et al. 1997). When measured on dimensions of social problem solving, social competence, social behaviour and social relations there was a moderate 10 per cent improvement, with a less impressive 5 per cent improvement in the symptoms of conduct disorder. Young offenders were found to be more likely to benefit from the training. It is important to note that the young offenders in this meta-analysis were older than the other groups, which could explain some of the difference in results. No effect was found on academic achievement.

The results of this meta-analysis do not support the use of social skills training as an intervention for treating behaviour disorders. The authors also found that, in some studies, comparison subjects did better than those enrolled in the social skills groups. It is important to note the potential sampling difficulties and that subjects were often selected on the basis of a social skills deficit rather than on the presence of an emotional or behaviour disorder. Many of the training programmes tested in these studies were designed for research, which tends to result in low external validity.

Anger management

Anger management is often offered in groups, and contains a stress reduction component (stress inoculation training). In this type of training, patients identify situations which cause anger and talk through solutions to reduce their own aggressive response to social cues. They are then taught relaxation techniques which they combine with the identified solutions. As in other CBT approaches, techniques are then practised in role-play facilitated by the anger management trainer.

A meta-analysis pooled the effects of 50 studies that looked at the impact of CBT on people's aggression. This found an overall positive effect. However, this review pooled effects across populations and treatment settings, which means that they included children, adults, young offenders, residential treatment, and community-based treatment in one overall effect size (Beck and Fernandez 1998). Another systematic review found four randomised trials specifically on anger management therapy for young people, but these were generally of poor quality or failed to show statistically significant differences in the treatment group. Whilst the treatment did not appear to produce harmful effects, the authors conclude that the effectiveness of anger control programmes was not demonstrated by the retrieved trials (Fonagy et al. 2002).

It has been suggested that anger coping programmes are more effective with those who are rejected by their peers, have internalising as well as externalising symptoms, and poor problem-solving skills (Lochman and Salekin 2003). However, this finding is based on programmes for younger children.

Aggression Replacement Training (ART) is a popular intervention used in the US. It was developed by Goldstein and Glick (1994), and builds on key techniques of cognitive behaviour therapy such as direct instruction, role-play and feedback. The programme uses these techniques in relation to ten specific scenarios: expressing a complaint, empathy, preparing for a stressful conversation, responding to anger, keeping out of fights, helping others, dealing with an accusation, dealing with group pressure, expressing affection, and responding to failure. The designers of this programme have reported mixed results from trials (Goldstein and Glick 1994).

Our search found no systematic review looking at the effectiveness of ART, but three individual studies were identified. One study found that ART reduced the rates of antisocial behaviour in a shelter for runaway young people, but this was a before–after study with no control group (Nugent, Bruley and Allen 1998). A second study, which was a randomised controlled trial, found only one statistically significant effect as a result of ART: improved knowledge of social skills (Coleman, Pfeiffer and Oakland 1992). In this study ART was delivered to a group of behaviour disordered young people in a residential treatment setting. In a more recent study in Norway, ART was found to improve behaviour and social skills in young people, some who had 'some degree of serious behaviour problems' (Gundersen and Svartdal 2006). However, this was not a randomised controlled trial, and it is not clear from the reporting whether any of the children were diagnosed with conduct disorder.

Moral reasoning training

Moral reasoning training aims to enhance conduct disordered young people's sense of fairness and justice in regards to other people's needs. Programme sessions focus on moral issues, for example through discussions (Fonagy et al. 2002).

A systematic review by Fonagy et al. (2002) found four studies that looked at the effect of moral reasoning training on children and young people's behaviour problems. The studies were well designed and carried out, but whilst two studies showed that the intervention group improved significantly more than the control group, the other two studies failed to show any effect (Fonagy et al. 2002). A promising approach tested out in one study was rational-emotive therapy (Block 1978), which is built on the idea that our emotional responses to situations derive from our interpretations of the situation rather than what actually happens. The therapy aims to teach young people how to think about themselves in a positive way, and how to have realistic expectations of themselves and others (Fonagy et al. 2002).

Cognitive behaviour therapy for conduct disorder and comorbid depression

One randomised controlled trial has looked at the effect of a cognitive behaviour therapy intervention delivered in a group format to young people with both depression and conduct disorder. The intervention used techniques from problem-solving and social skills programmes, whilst the comparison group received life skills training such as filling in job applications. At post-test assessment, the cognitive behaviour therapy group had significantly improved depression scores as compared to the life skills group, although no differences were found at 6- and 12-month follow-up. There were no significant differences between the groups in terms of conduct disorder at post-test or follow-up (Rhode *et al.* 2004).

Cognitive behaviour therapy has also been reported to be successful in Delhi, India, where a comparison study found the combination of CBT with parental counselling to be more effective in treating conduct disorder than CBT or parental counselling on its own, or compared to a waiting list control group (Broota and Sehgal 2004).

Cognitive behaviour therapy in the UK

A Youth Justice Board (YJB) evaluation was carried out in 2004, of 23 'cognitive behavioural' projects. These projects focused on the following aspects of CBT: moral reasoning; problem-solving techniques; interaction skills; self-management; prosocial modelling; patterns and consequences of offending behaviour; values, beliefs and thinking patterns; peers and assertion; and relapse prevention. Victim empathy and self-esteem were central themes. Some projects used motivational interviewing to prepare the young people for the CBT.

The evaluation was not able to establish the extent to which these projects were successful in reducing offending, or improving the young people's chances of stable education or work. However, there were lessons to be learned from these projects in terms of how to set up and run a CBT intervention:

- In total the CBT projects received 1446 referrals; of these, 1111 young people started on a project and 540 completed. Explanations for the high drop-out rate were that some young people were not adequately assessed before being referred, lack of time to implement the programme, and unwillingness on the part of the young people to comply with the demands that the project placed on them. High drop-out rates were particularly related to persistent young offenders, and contributed to the chaotic lifestyle of this client group.

- Projects that were designed according to research evidence, based on a clear rationale and included YOT practitioners in the developing phase were better understood and supported by staff and stakeholders.

- It was found to be essential for staff to be thoroughly trained in CBT theory and practice.

- Practitioners suggested that CBT needed to be integrated with practical support; according to one worker, '...it would be pointless for me to do a three-hour session with someone twice a week, and then the person's going to go back home and have no money, and want to go and steal for money' (Feilzer et al. 2004, p.33).

- One-to-one and group work were found not to be competing concepts but tended to complement each other.

The evaluators concluded that 'in order to make further progress with the development and implementation of cognitive behavioural projects, it would be advantageous to further develop those "cognitive behavioural" programmes which exhibited good practice to the point where they could be regarded as "demonstration projects" fit for accreditation' (Feilzer et al. 2004, p.61).

Conclusion

All plethora of different treatment programmes are based on the principle of cognitive behaviour therapy. Currently, there are mixed results from both individual studies and reviews as to the effectiveness of these approaches, and few rigorous systematic reviews have examined the effects of specific interventions, such as ART. The evidence is therefore inconclusive for all these interventions, and further research is needed. Poor descriptions of the programmes is also a problem, and some studies refer to the intervention in general terms of role-play, modelling, and behaviour modification, without examples of what this might entail (Broota and Sehgal 2004; Dush et al. 1989; Kavale et al. 1997).

Methods based on the principles of cognitive behaviour therapy are often used in systemic approaches, such as family therapy or therapeutic foster care. It may be that CBT on its own is unable to counteract influences from the wider community (family and school), but that it contributes to the effectiveness of systemic models.

8 Family and Parenting Interventions

Family and parenting interventions have gained support in recent years, partly as a result of promising research findings. There is evidence to support the overall effectiveness of parenting and family interventions, both in reducing offending and in the preventing and treating of conduct disorder (Barlow 1999; Chamberlain and Rosicky 1995; Dretzke *et al.* 2005; Farrington and Welsh 2002; Latimer 2001; Roberts and Camasso 1991; Woolfenden, Williams and Peat 2002).

A range of different parenting and family interventions are currently being promoted by various organisations, particularly for younger children. However, only some of these have been rigorously tested in randomised controlled trials, and some types have been found to be more effective than others (Barlow 1999; Liabo, Gibbs and Underdown 2004; Richardson and Joughin 2002). There is still a lack of knowledge as to which specific components of a programme are most crucial to its success. For adolescents, family therapy interventions targeting systemic factors (such as school, offending, marital problems) appear to be more effective than parent education programmes (Wolpert *et al.* 2006).

Family therapy

Family therapy aims to engage the child or adolescent and their family members in order to address problematic communication patterns, problems with discipline, and supervision. It is assumed that family interaction may cause, maintain or worsen conduct problems and thus family relationships are seen as a potent therapeutic agent (Woolfenden *et al.* 2002).

A systematic review of family therapy for children aged 10–17 with conduct problems was completed in 2001 (Woolfenden *et al.* 2002). This review focused on studies that included parent training interventions, family therapy, multisystemic therapy (MST) and multidimensional treatment foster care (MTFC). In seven of the included studies the participants were referred by juvenile justice systems in the US and were considered to be serious offenders. The remaining study included participants who had been assessed as having conduct disorder.

The results of the systematic review showed that:

- five of the included studies showed a decrease in the number of re-arrests for the young people who received family or parenting interventions compared to other treatment, although the authors warn that these results should be interpreted with caution because of the heterogeneity of the pooled data

- four studies found that family and parenting interventions significantly reduced the amount of time spent in institutions when compared with routine interventions

- there was insufficient evidence to conclude that family and parenting interventions have a beneficial effect on parenting, parental mental health, family functioning, academic performance, future employment, peer relations or future incarceration.

Strategic family therapy (SFT)

Strategic family therapy is similar in approach and theoretical background to family effectiveness training, structural family therapy and multidimensional family therapy. These interventions focus on the organisation of the family, its cohesion and structure.

Antisocial behaviour is assumed to result from malfunctioning family systems. The family system is seen as a system that attempts to maintain equilibrium – any changes within or external to the family are accompanied by shifts to achieve self-stabilisation. The aim of strategic family therapy is to alter family interactions, shared family beliefs and to reorganise family hierarchies and sub-systems and forms of emotional engagement.

A systematic review found promising results in studies on SFT, both at post-test and one-year follow-up (Fonagy *et al.* 2002). One of the studies found that both family functioning and child behaviour deteriorated in the individual child therapy group, whilst the SFT group improved on both of these measures (Szapocznik *et al.* 1989, quoted in Fonagy *et al.* 2002).

A more recent trial looked at the efficacy of brief strategic family therapy in reducing problem behaviour in conduct disordered Hispanic young people in comparison to a learning group intervention for young people only (Santisteban *et al.* 2003). In the family therapy group, all family members living in the household were asked to participate in the treatment, which was carried out in a clinic. Family therapy sessions were delivered on a weekly basis and participating families received between four and 20 hour-long sessions. The therapist took a very active role in guiding the family to adapt new ways of interacting. Overall, those who received family therapy improved significantly more than those receiving group therapy. More specifically, family therapy achieved significant improvement in terms of conduct disorder and socialised aggression. The study used a randomised controlled design, but an intention-to-treat analysis does not appear to have been carried out. Drop-out rates were similar in both intervention groups. The same authors achieved similar results in an earlier before–after study (Santisteban *et al.* 1997).

Two trials have found that brief strategic family therapy can reduce bullying behaviour in teenage girls (Nickel *et al.* 2006) and boys (Nickel *et al.* 2004). Considerable proportions of the samples were diagnosed with conduct disorder (approximately 35% of girls and 50% of boys). Family therapy was delivered over six months, and effects were sustained at one-year follow-up.

Functional family therapy (FFT)

Functional family therapy (FFT) sees young people's behaviour as serving a function in their family environment. The therapy aims to alter interactions and communication patterns to foster more adaptive functioning. Learning theory is also used in treatment in which attention is given to specific stimuli and responses to produce change.

In this type of treatment, the therapist highlights different aspects of the relationships between family members, in their normal functioning and in relation to the problem for which they sought therapy. It is believed that once the family is able to identify the problem and can see alternative ways of approaching it, they will be more likely to interact constructively; for example, increase positive reinforcement, clear communication and negotiations (Kazdin 2001).

A systematic review has found consistent evidence that FFT can significantly reduce offending and conduct problems in young people, including in relation to positive sibling behaviour (Fonagy *et al.* 2002). Research has also investigated specific treatment components of FFT. One study looked at therapist characteristics and found that relationship-building capacities such as warmth, affect–behaviour integration and humour accounted for almost half of the variability in predicting outcomes. A further 15 per cent variability was explained by the therapist's capacity to provide structure, such as being directive and having self-confidence (Alexander *et al.* 1976). A slightly different version of FFT (including education and job training) was shown to reduce re-offending rates of young people to 63 per cent, as compared to the 93 per cent re-offending within the control group. This is an important finding when considering the participants recruited to this study had previously been incarcerated and had conducted multiple offences (Barton *et al.* 1985).

However, despite such impressive research findings, the number of FFT practitioners available is limited. Fonagy *et al.* (2002) suggest that this could be linked to the considerable amount of training and supervision required in FFT, and the costs involved (an estimated US $2000/person). FFT was mentioned specifically in the Care Matters green paper, which suggested that a UK-based evaluation be carried out (Department for Education and Skills 2006a).

Multisystemic treatment (MST)

MST is one of the few developed and researched treatments specially designed for young people with conduct disorder, severe behaviour problems, or persistent young offenders. It was developed from the understanding that the range of the intervention strategies must extend alongside the range of causal factors that lead or contribute to conduct disorder. Thus interventions are delivered within the context of the family, school and community environment to reach several areas of the young person's environment (Henggeler and Borduin 1990; Henggeler, Schoenwald and Borduin 1998).

MST is a highly individualised treatment programme that integrates a variety of interventions. It is based on nine treatment principles:

1. *'Finding the fit'* between identified problems and their broader context.

2. Focus on the *positive* and use *strengths* identified in their immediate surroundings (e.g. family, neighbours, school) as levers for change.

3. Interventions are designed to *promote responsible behaviour and decrease irresponsible behaviour* among family members.

4. *Present-focused, action-oriented* and *well-defined* interventions.

5. Interventions target *sequences of behaviour* within and between multiple systems that maintain the identified problems.

6. Interventions fit the *developmental needs* of the young person.

7. Interventions are designed to require *continuous (daily or weekly) effort* from family members.

8. The effectiveness of interventions is *evaluated* continuously from multiple perspectives with providers assuming *accountability* for overcoming barriers to successful outcomes.

9. Interventions are designed to promote treatment *generalisation* and long-term maintenance of therapeutic change by empowering caregivers to address family members' needs across multiple systemic contexts.

MST addresses the alliances and sources of conflict in the family to change the young person's behaviour, their functioning in other systems, and the way their behaviour affects others. Owing to the broad focus of MST, many different treatment techniques are used, which may result in a package of interventions used with the young person and their family. The goals of treatment are:

- to help parents to develop positive and responsible behaviours of the young person

- to overcome marital difficulties that may hinder the parents' ability to function as parents

- to eliminate negative interactions between parents and the young person

- to build and develop cohesion and warmth among family members (Kazdin 2001).

In a recent Cochrane review, authors found no difference in treatment effect from MST compared with usual services (these were: residential care, arrests, convictions) (Littell 2005). This finding differs from those of a previous review (Curtis, Ronan and Borduin 2004), which found a statistically significant effect of MST over comparison treatments. When pooled from across studies of varying quality, results have tended to favour MST, but this was not replicated with more rigorous, intent-to-treat analyses (Littell 2005). At the same time, there is no research evidence that supports other interventions over MST. The Cochrane review points out that there are other aspects of this treatment model that may make it more attractive than some other services, such as placement in youth offending institutions. MST was not found to produce any harmful effects.

Woolfenden, Williams and Peat (2001) point out that MST is labour intensive and costly and that further research is required before these techniques can be widely adopted. However, where the alternative is institution, this is also a costly intervention. Studies have found that high treatment fidelity scores are associated with higher effects (Curtis *et al.* 2004; Ogden and Halliday-Boykins 2004; Schoenwald *et al.* 2003).

Multisystemic therapy in the UK

Apart from Cambridgeshire Youth Offending Service, the Brandon Centre, based in North London, is the only other service offering MST in Great Britain. In addition to MST, the Centre provides sexual health advice and contraception, and psychotherapy for young people aged 12 to 21 years. The Centre also runs a group-base parenting programme for parents of teenagers with behaviour problems.

The Brandon Centre has a tradition of combining service development with audit and research. Since 1993 the Centre has run an audit of its psychotherapy service. A study of attrition showed that young people with conduct problems were not engaging with the service. They tended to stop treatment unilaterally after just a few sessions (Baruch et al. 1998). Having tried one-to-one social skills and problem-solving skills training with some success, the Centre applied for funds to set up an MST service within a research trial. This was established in 2003 in partnership with Haringey Youth

Offending Service and Camden Youth Offending Team. The aim of the trial is to see whether MST is more effective than services as usual in preventing re-offending and custody among persistent young offenders. The trial is ongoing.

Therapist treatment adherence is a key feature of MST, and all MST projects have close ties with MST Services in the US. Therapists and supervisors attend a five-day training course arranged by MST Services in South Carolina. As part of the licence agreement with MST Services there is a weekly telephone consultation for the team with an MST consultant who also provides a quarterly booster training session for the teams from the Brandon Centre and Cambridgeshire Youth Offending Service.

MST therapists at the Brandon Centre have a background either in counselling psychology or social work, with experience of working in a youth offending service. The clinical supervisor is a psychologist and he works closely with each therapist to provide support and ensure treatment adherence. MST works intensively with young people and their families who typically have multiple problems in addition to the young people's problem behaviours. Due to the challenging aspects of the work, the caseload per therapist tends to be three to four families at any one time.

Parents are the key change agents in MST. The therapist helps parents set up a priority list for change, which is driven by their wishes, rather than the therapist's views. However, reducing offending behaviour is always a priority, and the therapist helps parents prioritise this amongst other problem behaviours. For example, going missing is a higher risk than a messy bedroom. Once risks and goals have been prioritised, the therapist works with parents to identify drivers for change in different systems (e.g. school, family, neighbourhood). When working with the family, the therapist uses a language of change, and emphasises a strategic approach. Amongst the techniques used are motivational interviewing with parents and behaviour contracting with the young people.

For more information see www.brandon-centre.org.uk and www.mstservices.com.

Parent management training (PMT)

PMT is based on social learning theory and assumes that conduct problems develop and are sustained by maladaptive parent–child interactions. The main aim of the training is to alter the interactive pattern between the parent and child so that prosocial rather than coercive behaviour is encouraged and reinforced in the family. Like other family interventions, PMT supports parents to establish clear rules and routines for children. Most programmes use videotapes to initiate discussions, as well as role-play exercises to help parents practise strategies taught (Mabe, Turner and Josephson 2001).

There are several variations of PMT, but the common characteristics of treatment include:

- treatment is conducted primarily with the parent(s)

- parents are trained to identify, define and observe problem behaviours in a different way

- parents are also trained to improve their communication with children, and to supervise and monitor behaviour

- the treatment sessions provide opportunities for parents to practise and refine the use of techniques taught, and see how they could be implemented

- progress at home is reviewed in the treatment sessions

- duration of the treatment ranges from 6 to 8 weeks for younger mildly oppositional children to 12 to 25 weeks for clinically referred conduct disordered children.

PMT has been shown to be more effective in younger children than adolescents (Fonagy et al. 2002). For example, Patterson, Dishion and Chamberlain (1993) found that PMT showed improvement in assessed behaviour in 36 per cent of children aged 3.5 to 6 years compared to 27 per cent of older children between the ages of 6 and 12. The decrease in effectiveness of parent management training can, in part, be explained by the fact that as children grow older, they become exposed to a wider array of social influences and are not solely reliant on their family. It is this recognition that has led clinicians to broaden the scope of therapeutic interventions for adolescents with conduct disorder (Patterson et al. 1993).

Woolfenden et al.'s (2001) review of family and parenting interventions in children with conduct problems aged 10–17 years included two studies on parent training. In one of these, parents were trained to identify a range of behaviours of their teenage children and to track and record them systematically. They were encouraged to discuss with their sons their daily movements and various behaviours and to keep in close liaison with their son's school. Behaviours were given consequences (both positive and restrictive) and parents were supported in the whole process by the therapeutic team. As a result, less time was spent in institutional care, which significantly reduced costs. An overall improvement in delinquent behaviours was also found. The long-term benefits reported from this programme are promising (Bank *et al.* 1991). Because parent management training treats families individually this is often reported under family therapy (Chamberlain and Rosicky 1995).

Another study included in the review by Woolfenden *et al.* (2001) looked at the effects of parent training on young people with conduct disorder, who had no involvement in the criminal justice system (Raue and Spence 1985). Two types of training programme were utilised: group parent reciprocity training and an individual-family-based reciprocity training programme. These treatments were both compared to a waiting list group. A decrease in problem behaviours in all groups occurred over time, but significantly more in the parenting treatment groups.

A Dutch study looked at the effectiveness of parent management training in combination with social problem-solving skills training for the children. The combination programme is called the Utrecht Coping Power Program (UCPP). This study only included children with clinical levels of behaviour problems, according to diagnostic criteria of the DSM-IV (APA 1994), including comorbidity with other problems. Families were randomised to either the UCPP or treatment as usual (mental health services offered by clinics, such as family therapy, psychotherapy and play therapy). Although there was a statistically significant difference in favour of UCCP immediately after treatment, this was not sustained at six-month follow-up when using an intention-to-treat analysis. This trial was accompanied by a cost-effectiveness study, which found UCPP to be more cost effective than treatment as usual (van de Wiel *et al.* 2003).

Foster care interventions

Compared with younger antisocial children, older delinquents are usually not only more aggressive, but their families are often distressed, demoralised, defeated or even cynical (Chamberlain and Reid 1998). The family may no longer be capable of supervising or negotiating with the young person. The young person becomes increasingly committed to and influenced by their delinquent peers, who in turn reinforce alienation and isolation from corrective adult influences. Eventually, when the behaviour of the young person significantly compromises the community's safety, the courts intervene and require that he or she be contained and held accountable. Parental supervision and guidance at this point is extremely important, and if the family is deemed incapable to provide this, their children may be placed outside the family home. Adolescents removed from their homes due to severe behaviour problems have traditionally been placed in either secure or community-based group care facilities.

In the UK, young people are placed in secure units, residential care units or foster homes. Lipsey and Wilson (1998) found that structured foster care programmes were effective in reducing re-offending in young people who had been institutionalised as a result of their offending behaviour. The intervention provided a group home for delinquents, which was run by a couple referred to as 'teaching parents'. These parents helped the young people with their behaviour skills and other problems in their lives, and monitored their progress in and outside school (Lipsey and Wilson 1998).

A Cochrane review has looked at the effect of cognitive behaviour therapy training programmes on foster carers' management of difficult behaviour. Five trials were included in the review, which did not find any evidence that such programmes improve outcomes for looked after young people (Turner, Macdonald and Dennis 2005). Outcomes looked at were psychological functioning, behaviour and interpersonal functioning. However, positive effects were found in the foster carers' behaviour management skills, attitudes and psychological functioning. A UK study has found that foster carers appreciated training, even though it did not impact on the young people's behaviour (Hill-Tout *et al.* 2003).

Multidimensional treatment foster care (MTFC)

Multidimensional treatment foster care uses the foster home as the primary site of therapeutic intervention and the treatment team is made up of both the foster carer(s) and the clinical team. Its theoretical framework is social learning theory, which sees young people's behaviour as a result of influences within their social context (family, school, peers, community). The model therefore intervenes across these settings, with foster carers (or treatment parents) as the primary change agents. Foster carers are provided with training and support services to design and implement interventions for the children in their home. The clinical team is responsible for helping children access community resources to facilitate their development and transition from the programme. Foster carers are available to the young person on a full-time basis, and are therefore paid a salary for their work (Reddy and Pfeiffer 1997; Shepard and Chamberlain 2005). They receive 24-hour support from the clinical team.

Behavioural expectations at home, school and in the community are well specified. A key aspect of MTFC is to keep the young person away from contacting other delinquents and to promote activities that will bring them into contact with more prosocial young people. The main mechanism for improving behaviour is a point system, whereby the young person is granted points for prosocial behaviour alongside clear-cut consequences for rule breaking.

MTFC has much in common with multisystemic therapy. Where the latter intervention aims to prevent the removal of the young person from their family home, MTFC aims to return the young person back to his or her family after an initial breakdown in relationships. Both interventions target multiple settings and determinants, both are delivered in community settings and both emphasise the importance of the parental (or foster carer) role in providing the young person with consistent and close supervision, and emotional involvement and support (Chamberlain and Reid 1998). In MTFC, daily treatment in the foster home is supplemented by the work of the clinical team who offer:

- individual therapy
- family therapy for the adolescent's biological or adoptive relatives
- regular school consultations including on-site observations and interventions as needed
- skills work to build their social competencies in the community
- psychiatric consultation as needed
- case management that coordinates all services and provides ongoing supervision and consultation to the foster parents (Chamberlain 1996).

Research utilising a matched comparison design and a randomised controlled trial has provided favourable evidence for the effectiveness of the MTFC intervention model (Chamberlain 1990; Chamberlain and Reid 1991). Woolfenden et al.'s (2001) systematic review includes Chamberlain and Reid's (1998) randomised controlled trial, which examined the effectiveness of MTFC compared with community group care among delinquents with an average of 14 previous criminal referrals. Boys ran away less frequently from MTFC than from group care, completed their programmes more often and were locked up in detention or training schools less frequently. MTFC boys also had fewer criminal referrals from the time that they were placed in care through to the year after discharge from the programmes. Self-report on delinquent acts and violent or serious crimes was also lower for this group (Chamberlain and Reid 1998). Furthermore, a follow-up of this study found that these outcomes were sustained two years after treatment completion (Eddy, Whaley and Chamberlain 2004). These findings were mirrored in a review of foster care interventions (Hahn *et al.* 2004).

A pilot study has looked at completion rates with MTFC for boys and girls. Although treatment results appeared similar for both genders, there was an increase in rates of girls' conduct problems during the first six months of treatment, whilst in the same time period boys' rates fell slightly. The programme developers concluded that the model needed to be gender adapted, to help foster carers deal with girls' more passive patterns of aggressive behaviour such as spreading rumours, being bossy, and rolling eyes in response to directives. Although preliminary findings indicate that these adaptations have improved MTFC for girls, some risk behaviours are persisting. The programme developers at the Oregon Social Learning Center are continuing to revise the model to meet the specific needs of girls (Shepard and Chamberlain 2005).

Multidimensional treatment foster care in the UK

In January 2005, the Department for Education and Skills (DfES) announced a special grant for the development of multidimensional treatment foster care in England (MTFCE). The programme is intended for young people who are difficult to place due to their challenging behaviour, and for whom the alternative is likely to be secure residential placements. MTFC has previously been tried with young offenders, whereas in England there is a focus on young people in local authority care. This means that not all of the young people will be going to their birth families after treatment completion, but will require continued foster care or adoption.

The English programme uses the framework developed by the Oregon Social Learning Center, which is based on social learning theory. However, the model is flexible within this framework and delivery has been adapted to fit with local circumstances. A key development in England is that teams employ an education worker to focus specifically on issues in relation to school. MTFCE teams also employ a programme manager, usually a social worker, who serves as a link between the project and the wider system. Clinical management and supervision is undertaken by specially trained staff; usually psychologists or social workers. In general, however, MTFCE does not appoint people according to their professions, but in relation to the skills needed in the team.

Developmental support, training and consultation are provided by the South London and Maudsley NHS Trust and Central Manchester and Manchester University Children's Hospitals Trust, and the national evaluation will be carried out by the Social Work Research and Development Unit at the University of York: www.york.ac.uk/inst/swrdu/Projects/tfc.html).

For more information about MTFC see www.oslc.org.

Barriers to successful family-based treatments

Several studies have shown that multiple personal and environmental stressors experienced by family members, particularly parents, prevent them from benefiting from treatment, and present problems for programme implementation (Dumas and Wahler 1983; McMahon and Forehand 1984; Patterson 1982). Effectiveness has been associated with two specific family variables (Chamberlain and Rosicky 1995).

1. *Attrition*
    Families who drop out of treatment have been found to be of lower socio-economic status, have mothers who are more depressed and to be agency (versus self) referred. Higher success has been reported when participants are under 15 years of age (Latimer 2001). Families who drop out have been found to be those whose children and adolescents have a greater number of symptoms of conduct disorder and delinquency, lower educational and occupational status and lower income. Drop-out rates of over 50 per cent have been reported in

treatment studies of families of conduct disordered young people (Kazdin, Holland and Crowley 1997).

'Family resistance' once in treatment has also been identified as a significant barrier. Some parents may disapprove of the parenting strategies promoted, or lack the means or time to implement them (Keegan Eamon and Venkataraman 2003). Parents may also feel that the main problem lies within the child rather than their own parenting practices (Peters, Calam and Harrington 2005). The application of strategic/structural family systems engagement strategies has been found to significantly improve initial engagement rates.

2. *Family stress and lack of social support*
    The probability of treatment failure steadily increased as a function of low socio-economic status, social isolation or both. The relationship between poverty and effectiveness of family interventions appears to be similar to the relationship between poverty and behaviour problems in children – high levels of stress, parental depression, marital discord, low social support, and residence in disadvantaged areas (Keegan Eamon and Venkataraman 2003; Peters *et al.* 2005).

    The inclusion of specific components designed to enhance social support has been found to increase effectiveness. However, this has been found with families of younger children and may not be applicable to adolescent populations.

    Capaldi and Patterson (1987) found that the use of home visits to explain the nature of programmes and the importance of parent involvement, incentives for participation, and frequent reminders increased parent participation from 35 per cent to 78 per cent (Capaldi and Patterson 1987).

Conclusion

Family interventions for conduct disordered young people have been extensively researched, and findings so far are promising. However, we do not currently know which of these programmes are the most effective, for whom, and whether they are likely to produce better results than usual services. Fortunately, UK government initiatives in 2005 and 2006 may address some gaps in the evidence, particularly in relation to FFT and MTFC (Department for Education and Skills 2006a).

One review has found that programmes treating the whole family, including the young person, were effective, whereas parent training programmes were not (Fonagy *et al.* 2002). The Cochrane review on MST is a good example of how rigorous analysis can alter previous conclusions of the effectiveness of interventions (Littell 2005). At present, reviews of the same quality are not available for other types of parenting and family interventions, although a Cochrane review on treatment foster care is in progress (Turner and Macdonald 2006).

Whilst the research evidence is inconclusive, there are ethical reasons for choosing family treatment programmes over other interventions. Young people themselves have said in consultations that they generally prefer to stay with their family rather than being removed from the home (Department for Education and Skills 2006a). Furthermore, if parents are provided tools to deal with difficult behaviour, this may have an impact on younger siblings in the future.

Research has identified several reasons why some parents find it difficult to attend parenting groups. Therapists' attitudes and competencies may also play an important part in determining outcomes, but at present there is little research looking at this variable (Liabo *et al.* 2004).

9 School-based Interventions

Children and young people spend a lot of their time in school, where anti-social behaviour manifests itself in terms of truanting, exclusions and bullying. A survey carried out in the UK in 1998 found that approximately 30 per cent of school exclusions are due to bullying, fighting and assault on peers. Seventeen per cent is due to disruption, misconduct and unacceptable behaviour, whereas approximately 1 per cent is due to physical abuse and assault on staff (Social Exclusion Unit 1998). Although school-based interventions are unlikely to be enough to treat conduct disorder at an individual level, interventions implemented during school hours may help prevent problems escalating, and reduce violence within peer groups. Research evidence supports the use of systemic interventions, where the police, social services and primary carers collaborate to impact positively on a young person's behaviour. Schools have an important role to play in such collaborations, and programmes implemented to change the social environment at school can help facilitate individual support.

At a strategic level, one systematic review of school-based crime prevention programmes found research evidence to support the implementation of four main strategies (Gottfredson *et al.* 2002):

1. building school capacity to support effective management. Establishing and enforcing school rules, policies, or regulations to manage discipline

2. establishing norms or expectations for behaviour

3.   changing management and teaching practices in the classroom to improve learning and the social environment

4.   grouping students in different ways to achieve smaller, less alienating or otherwise more suitable micro-climates within the school.

The review included evaluations that used a control group, and which looked at offending, substance misuse, education and behaviour problems outcomes. The four principles outlined above were found to impact positively on school attendance and substance use, but with mixed effects on antisocial behaviour and crime.

A well-known school-based approach is the Olweus anti-bullying programme. It is delivered across the whole school, and focuses on increasing the awareness and reaction to bullying amongst students, parents, teachers and school staff. A school conference day is arranged to set bullying on the agenda. The school environment is changed by increased supervision during recess and lunch time, anti-bullying rules agreed within each class and regular meetings with students. Links are set up with specialist services, such as social workers and school psychologists, to deal with the most severe cases. The programme is designed to be delivered within the existing school structure, by teachers and other employees. However, it also draws on experts such as social workers and psychotherapists in relation to persistent and serious bullies (Olweus 1994).

The programme was initially developed and evaluated in Norway, using a case control design. Bullying behaviour four months before the programme was compared with bullying behaviour after programme implementation. The sample was large (n = 2500 approximately), but the study did not include a control group (apart from the group measured four months before implementation). This initial evaluation found substantial reductions in bullying behaviour (Olweus 1991); however, this was not replicated in a later study which even found some evidence of increased bullying (Roland 1993). The Olweus programme has been adapted elsewhere and modified versions have been evaluated in controlled studies in Belgium and Finland, showing some reduction in bullying. A before–after study in Canada did not find any effect from the programme (Rigby 2002).

A modified version of the Olweus bullying programme has also been evaluated in the UK (Smith and Sharp 1994). This study used a control group, and found a reduction in reported bullying. One difference from the Olweus model was that many schools in the UK focused more on problem-solving techniques and consensus than rules and supervision. A controlled study in Spain made similar adaptations and found a reduction in bullying frequency (Ortega and Lera 2000; Rigby 2002). Across all evaluations it appears that involving the school in the implementation increases the programme's effectiveness (Rigby 2002).

A meta-analysis has found that school-based interventions are effective in reducing disruptive behaviour in the classroom, when measured by observation. Teacher-report measures did not yield statistically significant results. Programmes delivered to children in separate classes were more effective than those delivered in regular classroom settings (Stage and Quiroz 1997). This analysis was not based on a comprehensive search and included a range of different types of studies, such as single-case studies and time series. Excluded from the analysis were studies using standardised behaviour measuring scales such as the Child Behavior Checklist. The limited search and inclusion criteria weaken the relevance of these results.

Some school-based interventions target specifically young people who exhibit, or are at risk of exhibiting, problem behaviour. Programmes generally fall within three main categories, but will typically consist of elements across the three (Stage and Quiroz 1997):

- Behavioural interventions such as token economies where you earn benefits from positive behaviour, or where benefits are withdrawn in response to negative behaviour. Punishment such as isolation, or being taken away from a group activity, and the use of report cards to main carers also fall within the category of behavioural strategies.

- Cognitive behavioural interventions delivered in school are similar to those delivered in clinic or youth centre settings and may include anger control, relaxation and social problem solving. At school these techniques may also include training of well-behaved peers, to help them support their class mates to engage in prosocial behaviour, or to react against antisocial activities.

- Individual counselling may be used in school settings, either via school psychologists, or by training teachers.

A systematic review of targeted school-based violence prevention programmes found that these were effective in reducing aggression and violence in both primary and secondary schools. The review included 56 individual studies, which were all randomised controlled trials. Seven studies looked at outcomes after 12 months and found that the effect was maintained. The types of programmes fell into two main categories:

1.   programmes teaching children problem-solving skills/anger control

2.   programmes either teaching relationship skills or intervening in the social context.

Programmes included in the review were delivered specifically to children who were aggressive, or considered to be at risk of developing aggressive behaviour. Programmes that taught children relationship or social skills were more effective than those that taught children not to respond in pro-vocative situations. However, statistically significant benefits were found for both types of programmes (Mytton *et al.* 2006). The review was based on a comprehensive search strategy and careful meta-analysis, which strengthens the results.

Another more recent systematic review also focused on interventions in school for children at risk of, or already displaying, antisocial behaviour. This review looked at evaluations of social-information processing programmes. These are similar to those in category 1 above, and focus on children's thinking skills in provocative situations, for example how they interpret and respond to social cues. Programmes that focused on behaviour training were excluded. The review found an overall positive effect on aggressive behaviour, and recommends these programmes for implementation in primary and secondary schools. The effect was consis-tent across different programme models (Wilson and Lipsey 2006b). A systematic review by the same authors looked at these programmes' effect when delivered universally to all children in a school or classroom (Wilson and Lipsey 2006a). Again, an overall positive effect on aggression was found.

Some young people who are excluded from mainstream school are offered places in alternative education settings. One review of such programmes found that these interventions did not have a statistically sig-nificant effect on delinquency or school performance. Small but positive effects were observed in relation to school attitude and self-esteem, also important outcomes for young people who have been excluded from the mainstream the education system (Cox, Davidson and Bynum 1995).

School-based interventions – an example from the UK

A school-based social work intervention was set up in two schools in Dorset, one primary and one secondary school within the same catchment area. The intervention was managed by a senior education welfare officer, who worked directly with children and their families. In the primary school he was assisted by a full-time project teacher. In the secondary school a part-time project teacher delivered health education with a focus on substance abuse prevention.

The education welfare officer received referrals, mainly from teachers, when a child exhibited antisocial behaviour at school. The focus of the intervention was on eight specific areas:

1. family and child counselling, based on cognitive behaviour principles

2. child protection issues

3. transition to secondary school, which included a pre-transfer counselling session for children in the primary school

4. bullying, using the Olweus anti-bullying programme and in the secondary school including conferences for all identified cases. The conferences would include victims, perpetrators and sometimes their families or school class

5. truanting, which focused both on creating a dialogue with parents and addressing reasons for truanting, such as bullying

6. health education

7. community development and inter-agency collaboration, which included weekly meetings with representatives from probation, police, social work, housing, community work and school health services

8. school exclusion, with the educational welfare officer working collaboratively with teachers to reduce pressures that contribute to negative behaviour.

After three years the intervention appeared to have reduced bullying and theft in the primary school, where there was a drop in both these behaviours. Bullying and theft increased in the control school during the same period. In secondary school the intervention appeared to reduce theft, truanting, fights and use of hard drugs. On the other hand, bullying increased by 20 per cent in the intervention school whereas it fell by 7 per cent in the control school.

Qualitative interviews with children and parents found them to be enthusiastic about the intervention which they felt had been personal, individually tailored and confidential. A particularly positive aspect of the service was the immediacy of the response, and the education welfare officer often saw the family the same day as the problem was brought to attention. Whilst in the beginning the caseload was characterised by crisis interventions, this later changed to preventive strategies. Teacher morale was boosted in the intervention schools, who felt more positive towards handling difficult behaviour, and the intake of children with learning or behaviour difficulties increased.

This pilot evaluation overall produced promising results. The results must be interpreted in light of the methodological weaknesses of the comparison design; most notably this was a small study, there was no randomisation, and the two primary schools differed on key characteristics. The rise in bullying in the intervention secondary school is also of concern. At the same time there were other very positive outcomes. This is a relatively cheap intervention. The 2.5 salaried workers cost £187,875 in 1998 prices over three years (Bagley and Pritchard 1998; Pritchard 2001).

Conclusion

Evaluations of school-based programmes to reduce bullying and antisocial behaviour indicate that school is an arena where interventions can work. There is some evidence to support school-wide anti-bullying programmes. The Olweus anti-bullying programme has been adapted across different countries and found to be a promising intervention, but other models have also been successful. It is recognised that bullying behaviour is difficult to change, and although some evaluations have found impressive results, the effects are overall modest, but positive (Rigby 2002). More effective programmes tend to be grounded in theory and be well implemented (Stevens, De Bourdeaudhuij and Van Oost 2001).

Two high-quality systematic reviews have found that targeted interventions for young people at risk of developing, or already exhibiting, antisocial behaviour are effective in reducing such behaviour. Interventions that focus on relationship and social skills appear more effective than those teaching children how to respond to provocative situations, although both types of programme are supported by the evidence (Mytton *et al.* 2006; Wilson and Lipsey 2006b).

10 Pharmacology

Psychopharmacological treatment is rarely used in UK settings. Most of the research has been carried out in the US and, at present, there are few rigorous studies to support the use of any agent (Fonagy *et al.* 2002; Harrington and Bailey 2003; Wolpert *et al.* 2006). Furthermore, treatment regimes tested in research studies have generally not been replicated in practice-based trials.

Considering the lack of robust research in this field, this review does not give details of treatment regimes for any medication.

Psychopharmacological interventions mostly target comorbid conditions and their specific symptoms such as ADHD, and occasionally bipolar disorder (Fonagy *et al.* 2002; Marriage, Fine and Moretti 1986).

Psychostimulants

The term psychostimulants, or stimulants, refers to a class of drugs that includes Ritalin, dexamphetamine, and combinations of dextro and levo amphetamine (Adderall). Pemoline is no longer licensed due to dangerous side effects on the liver. Psychostimulants have been found to be effective in the treatment of ADHD, and may help for conduct disorder where ADHD is present. There is an overlap in the symptoms of conduct disorder and ADHD in that both have impulsivity (Gérardin *et al.* 2002). However, few studies have looked at this group (Fonagy *et al.* 2002) and one review reported mixed findings (Bassarath 2003). It has been suggested that the effect of psychostimulants may be dose-dependent, and that it is more suitable for treating mild but not severe forms of aggression (Campbell, Cueva and Adams 1999; Campbell, Gonzalez and Silva 1992).

Three reviews of the literature in this field found that psychostimulants have overall been shown to be effective in reducing antisocial behaviours in comorbid conduct disorder and ADHD in adolescents, even when excluding the effects on attention-deficit and hyperactivity symptoms (Fonagy *et al.* 2002; Gérardin *et al.* 2002; Steiner, Saxena and Chang 2003). All of the relevant studies had looked specifically at methylphenidate and mostly in comparison with placebo. One study looked at methylphenidate in comparison with clonidine, and found that the two agents had similar effects on aggression in comorbid ADHD and oppositional defiant disorder or conduct disorder (Connor, Barkley and Davis 2000).

A double-blind placebo-controlled trial conducted after the above reviews looked at the use of pemoline in conduct disordered young people with comorbid ADHD and substance misuse. Pemoline was found to significantly reduce hyperactivity, but not conduct disorder or substance misuse (Riggs, Mikulich and Hall 2001).

Neuroleptics

Neuroleptics are the most commonly used psychotropic drugs in the treatment of severe aggression in children and adolescents, particularly those with chronic problems who are hospitalised (Campbell *et al.* 1992; Gérardin *et al.* 2002). Drugs included in this category are haloperidol, pimozide, molindone, thioridazine, chlorpromazine, and risperidone. The literature is inconclusive on whether neuroleptics have anti-aggressive properties per se or whether the effect seen is a result of sedative properties (Gérardin *et al.* 2002).

Two reviews have concluded that whilst neuroleptics have been shown to reduce aggressiveness, effects are associated with sedation and interference with learning as well as more severe side effects including those of extrapyramidal character, neuroleptic malignant syndrome, dyskinesias and tardive dystonia (Fonagy *et al.* 2002; Gérardin *et al.* 2002). Molindone, thioridazine and the atypical antipsychotic clozapine have been found to reduce aggression, but poor study designs weaken the reliability of these results (Fonagy *et al.* 2002). Risperidone, another atypical antipsychotic, has been found to have a role in the treatment of aggression in non-psychotic patients, and some see risperidone as the first line of atypical antipsychotic medication (Steiner *et al.* 2003; Toren, Laor and Weizman 1998). However, there is a lack of double-blind placebo-controlled trials for this drug, apart from two carried out with learning disabled children

(Cheng-Shannon *et al.* 2004; Findling *et al.* 2003; Fonagy *et al.* 2002). There is some evidence that haloperidol is effective in acute situations of severe and explosive aggression, but again there is a lack of high-quality studies on its effect on conduct disordered young people (Steiner *et al.* 2003). One study has suggested that haloperidol has more side effects than lithium and is less effective (Platt *et al.* 1984).

An open-label, before–after study looking at the effects of risperidone was published after the completion of the above reviews. The findings supported the use of risperidone to treat conduct disorder in children and adolescents, but the small sample size (n = 21) and study design weaken the results and their generalisability (Ercan *et al.* 2003). A further study examining risperidone looked at prolactin levels during long-term treatment of conduct disorder in learning disabled children and young people (IQ score ≥ 36 and ≤ 84). This study found that although prolactin levels increased considerably in weeks 4–7 of treatment, it subsequently fell in weeks 40–48 and weeks 52–55, to within the normal range, although the average was still about twice as high as it had been at the start of the study (Findling *et al.* 2003).

Reyes *et al.* (2006) carried out an international, randomised, double-blind, placebo-controlled study of risperidone as a maintenance treatment in children who originally responded well in an open-label part of the study. They found that participants on risperidone had a longer time to symptom recurrence than those on placebo. The study also indicated that symptoms deteriorated for all subjects (on average), although less for those on risperidone (Reyes *et al.* 2006).

Lithium carbonate

Lithium is a recognised treatment for bipolar disorder in adults. It therefore theoretically has been thought useful for children and adolescents who have explosive mood problems. It requires a strict treatment protocol and has been associated with serious side effects (Fonagy *et al.* 2002; Gérardin *et al.* 2002). Four reviews have found lithium to be an effective intervention in the treatment of aggression in conduct disorder. However, they do not recommend use unless the young person is an inpatient or the parents are able to exercise strict control over the treatment, and only as a last resort when other treatments have failed (Bassarath 2003; Fonagy *et al.* 2002; Gérardin *et al.* 2002; Steiner *et al.* 2003). It is important to note that although reviews of the literature have found overall effectiveness from lithium, some single studies have not. Fonagy *et al.* (2002) note that types of aggression appear to be critical determinants of effectiveness, with lithium being more effective for severe and explosive aggression. Length of treatment has also been reported as an important variable in effective treatment, as lithium tends to become effective within two to four weeks, when therapeutic serum levels are reached (Fonagy *et al.* 2002; Steiner *et al.* 2003).

The common side effects associated with lithium are stomach ache, tremor of the hands, headache, polyuria and weight gain. Other reported side effects include exacerbation of acne, deposition of lithium in bones, hypothyroidism, muscular weakness, leukocytosis, thrombocytosis and nephrotic syndrome (Werry 1997).

Anticonvulsants

Anticonvulsants have been used to target rage outbursts, especially where a seizure disorder is suspected (Lavin and Rifkin 1993). Drugs belonging to the group anticonvulsants are diphenylhydantoin, carbamazepine and divalproex sodium.

Carbamazepine has been suggested for this population because it is believed that aggression in conduct disorder may be caused by abnormal electrical activity in the temporal lobe (Fonagy *et al.* 2002). Evidence to support its effectiveness is, however, lacking. Two reviews found that although open trials report positive effects from carbamazepine on aggression in conduct disorder, double-blind placebo-controlled trials have been unable to replicate these results (Fonagy *et al.* 2002; Gérardin *et al.* 2002).

Sodium valproate is a branched-chain carboxylic acid (Gérardin *et al.* 2002). It has a wider therapeutic window than lithium, and it has therefore been suggested that it may be appropriate for adolescents who are less compliant, harder to supervise and potentially abusing street drugs (Steiner *et al.* 2003). The term 'therapeutic window' is related to how strict (or narrow) the treatment regime needs to be, in order to provide a safe treatment.

Three reviews have found some research that supports the use of divalproex sodium, which contains sodium valproate and valproic acid, to reduce explosive aggression in conduct disordered children aged 6–14 years (Fonagy *et al.* 2002; Gérardin *et al.* 2002; Steiner *et al.* 2003). The reviews found one open trial and one small double-blind placebo-controlled follow-up trial of 20 outpatients.

Other compounds

Clonidine is now recognised as a second-line treatment for ADHD, and so may help conduct problems in the presence of ADHD. It has also occasionally been used for children with conduct disorder only. Three reviews found that the effect of this drug had only been investigated in open-label trials, but that the results from these were promising (Fonagy *et al.* 2002; Gérardin *et al.* 2002; Steiner *et al.* 2003). Teacher reports indicated that clonidine reduced explosive aggression and the children seemed to be more readily accepted by peers when on a course of this medication.

One blinded randomised controlled trial published after the above reviews looked at the effects of clonidine on aggression and hyperactivity in children aged 6–14 with comorbid ADHD and conduct disorder or oppositional defiant disorder, who were already on psychostimulants. Clonidine was provided to children aged 6–14 years, in addition to the ongoing psychostimulant therapy, and was compared with placebo. At six weeks post-test, clonidine was found to significantly improve conduct but not hyperactivity, as measured by parent report. Missing data were a problem in this study: 78 per cent of subjects had some missing data points (Hazell and Stuart 2003).

The most severe side effects reported for clonidine were drowsiness and dizziness (Fonagy *et al.* 2002; Hazell and Stuart 2003). According to parental report, side effects decreased over time and included 'talks less to others', 'uninterested in others', 'irritable', 'prone to crying', and 'anxious' (Hazell and Stuart 2003).

Three reviews looked at the research evidence for selective serotonin reuptake inhibitors in the treatment of aggression in young people with conduct disorder, but found no good quality studies that support this line of treatment (Fonagy *et al.* 2002; Gérardin *et al.* 2002; Steiner *et al.* 2003). Similarly, no research evidence was found to support the use of beta-blockers or minor tranquillisers (Fonagy *et al.* 2002; Steiner *et al.* 2003).

Conclusion

Research evidence to date does not support the use of any pharmacological agent for conduct disordered young people. Although some trials present promising results, these have not been replicated in practice settings, and some of the side effects are severe. There is some research evidence to support the use of methylphenidate for comorbid ADHD and conduct disorder.

Ethical implications of the use of pharmacological treatments have not been discussed here, but need to be considered should further, more rigorous, research become available.

11 Interventions for Young People Involved in Fire-setting and Arson

Our search strategy did not find any systematic review of interventions for young people involved in arson or firesetting. The search retrieved one comprehensive literature review and one effectiveness study. This could be because arson is a relatively rare type of behaviour, and most studies therefore include a wide age span, and mainly younger children.

The literature review concluded that programmes tend to fall within two categories: educational programmes and those based on cognitive behaviour therapy. However, there is a lack of rigorous studies that address the effectiveness of these interventions. The review was accompanied by a UK-based survey of organisations involved in delivering interventions to young firesetters. Although valuable initiatives were identified, the study concluded that there is an overall lack of adherence to principles of good practice developed for this field (Palmer, Caulfield and Hollin 2005).

The effectiveness study evaluated an intervention called the Trauma Burn Outreach Prevention Program (TBOPP). This consists of a one-day course for young people and their parents, which focuses on the medical, financial, legal and societal impact of firesetting with an emphasis on individual accountability and responsibility. Only one young person engaged in firesetting after participating in the programme (representing a recidivism rate of 0.8%). This was compared to the recidivism of a sample of firesetters and arsonists who had not participated where the rate was 36 per cent (Franklin *et al.* 2002). However, it is not clear from the reporting whether the two groups were similar at the start of the programme, and the differences in outcomes could be due to differences between the two groups from the start. The programme was delivered to children and young people aged 4–17 years (mean age across both groups was 12 years).

Two other additional trials were found that aimed to address arson and firesetting, but their samples appeared to have included mainly younger children. One of these (n = 138) did not find any significant effects from an education and behaviour programme delivered by fire fighters (Adler *et al.* 1994). The children in this study averaged eight years of age, but the programme was delivered to those aged between 5 and 16 years. A small study by Kolko (n = 54) supported both a CBT intervention and an education programme over a one-off home visit by a fire fighter. This programme was delivered to children aged 5–13 years, with an average age of 9.6 years (Kolko 2001). The lack of effectiveness interventions for this population has been identified in other reviews (Barreto *et al.* 2004; Hoover 2003).

12 Other Treatments for Conduct Disorder

This book presents interventions that have been evaluated by research. In addition there are many interventions and services for which the effectiveness is unknown, simply because little research has been undertaken.

There is increasing interest in the role that diet, or vitamin supplements, can play in managing difficult behaviour. Research in this field is promising, but still in its pilot phase (Gesch *et al.* 2002; Kaplan *et al.* 2004; Liu *et al.* 2004). No intervention trials were found that fulfilled our inclusion criteria.

At present, a Cochrane protocol has been registered for a systematic review on *Exercise for Oppositional Defiant Disorder and Conduct Disorder in Children and Adolescents* (Ekeland *et al.* 2006). However, our searches did not identify any studies that evaluated sport interventions for conduct disorder.

13 Treatment Approaches for Young Offenders

Not all young offenders have a conduct disorder, and not all conduct disordered young people will be offenders, although given the diagnostic criteria for the disorder, a link is likely in practice. Several of the criteria set by the ICD-10 and DSM-IV classifications (WHO 1994; APA 1994) include offending behaviours such as stealing and cruelty to others. Key to a diagnosis of conduct disorder is that the young person has a repetitive and persistent pattern of behaviour 'in which either the basic rights of others or major age-appropriate societal norms or rules are violated' over a six-month period (World Health Organization 1993). It is because of this overlap in populations that we now turn to the research evidence on interventions to prevent re-offending in delinquent young people.

This chapter is based on findings from reviews and meta-analyses, retrieved in an additional search to that carried out specific to interventions for the management of conduct disorder. This chapter draws out the main messages from research on interventions to reduce youth offending.

The Research Evidence

Thirty-two reviews were found that fulfilled the inclusion/exclusion criteria (Adams 2003; Andrews *et al.* 1990; Antonowicz and Ross 1994; Bedard *et al.* 2003; Brewer *et al.* 1995; Chamberlain and Rosicky 1995; Coffey and Gemignani 1994; Cox *et al.* 1995; Dowden and Andrews

2003, 2004; Farrington and Welsh 2002; Gottfredson *et al.* 2002; Izzo and Ross 1990; Kurtz 2002; Latimer 2001; Layton MacKenzie 2002; Lees, Manning and Rawlings 2004; Lipsey 1992, 1995; Lipsey, Chapman and Landenberger 2001; Lipsey and Wilson 1998; McLaren 1992; Petrosino 1997; Petrosino, Turpin-Petrosino and Buehler 2004; Poyner 1993; Redondo, Sanchez-Meca and Garrido 1999; Roberts and Camasso 1991; Sutton 2002; Welsh and Hoshi 2002; Wilson and Lipsey 2000; Wilson, Lipsey and Soydan 2003; Woolfenden *et al.* 2001). This literature gives pointers to the main types of interventions that may help reduce offending behaviour, but in general, detailed information on service content is lacking, as is information on the characteristics of the young people included, and the type of offences that were reduced. Meta-analysis is a powerful way of combining results from a range of studies, but unless used with appropriate caution, this method has the potential to cover up weaknesses in study design, and compare studies that are quite different in approach. For example, some reviews combine effectiveness of adult interventions with those for young people.

Nevertheless, certain characteristics were identified across studies as being important when designing effective interventions for young offenders.

- Approaches based on cognitive and/or behaviour therapy have been found to contribute to reducing offending rates across a variety of programmes (Lipsey *et al.* 2001; Redondo *et al.* 1999). One review found that the most successful programmes were aimed at changing how young offenders think, as well as how they behave and feel (Izzo and Ross 1990).

- The most successful programmes target direct causes of offending behaviour, rather than underlying causes (Izzo and Ross 1990; Kurtz 2002; Lipsey 1992; Redondo *et al.* 1999). One review found that 90 per cent of successful interventions targeted these causes compared with 58 per cent of the unsuccessful ones (Antonowicz and Ross 1994). Direct causes are things like the young person's offending behaviour, antisocial behaviour, attitudes or feelings, antisocial peer associations, lack of non-criminal role models, poor problem-solving skills, and issues related to his or her family.

- The use of core correctional practice has been linked to more positive results (Dowden and Andrews 2004), defined as the adherence by staff to five key principles:

1. effective use of authority, defined as unambiguous rules and positive reinforcement of them

2. modelling and positive reinforcement of anti-criminal attitudes and behaviour

3. teaching of concrete problem-solving skills

4. active involvement by correctional staff in arranging community services for the offenders

5. establishing conditions with open, warm and enthusiastic communication between staff and offenders.

- Mainstream programmes for juvenile offenders have been found to be as effective for minority ethnic groups (Wilson *et al.* 2003).

- Services that incorporate a variety of treatments appear to be more effective than those relying on one single technique (Kurtz 2002; Lipsey and Wilson 1998). One review found that 70 per cent of successful programmes were multifaceted compared with only 38 per cent of those that were unsuccessful (Antonowicz and Ross 1994).

Some characteristics of the evaluation methodology or reporting were found to impact on the identified programme effect. Studies where the researchers were highly involved in the delivery of service produced higher effects than when researchers were less involved (Lipsey *et al.* 2001; Wilson *et al.* 2003) and unpublished work reported smaller effects than those published in journals, books or dissertations (Wilson *et al.* 2003). When the investigators were blinded during data collection this was also found to produce smaller effects (Wilson *et al.* 2003).

Lipsey (1992) has performed one of the largest meta-analyses to date. His review contains over 400 studies and his selection can be assumed to cover almost all the samples in early meta-analysis of juvenile delinquency. However, the majority of the studies assessed come from North America or Anglo-American countries, and the question of generalisability still has to be tested empirically.

There are problems of heterogeneity in Lipsey's (1992) meta-analysis because it contains studies on a wide variety of treatments, for different kinds of problems. These include studies on sentenced offenders, young people that display antisocial behaviour and children at risk. This raises the concern that results could be generalised inappropriately.

Lipsey (1992) found:

- structured and focused approaches, such as behavioural and skills-oriented treatments, and multifaceted programmes were more effective than the less structured approaches, such as counselling

- the more structured treatment types reduced re-offending rates in the range of 10–20 per cent, when used both inside and outside the juvenile justice system

- a couple of treatment categories appeared to produce negative effects, most noticeably the deterrence treatments – this included shock incarceration and the 'scared straight' programme model, which includes organised visits to prisons for young offenders or those at risk of becoming involved in offending.

Lipsey (1995) provides further discussion of the meta-analysis. Major points include:

- Characteristics such as age, ethnicity and prior arrest history are related to treatment effects. A general pattern is that offending behaviour is reduced more in young people of higher risk or severity than those of lower risk.

- Treatment in the juvenile justice system was associated with slightly smaller effects than those provided by other agencies, although the difference was small.

- When treatment type is taken into account, the same pattern is found in both juvenile justice and non-juvenile justice systems. Behavioural or skills-oriented programmes have the most effect on the young people's behaviour.

The following sections present research evidence on different interventions, organised according to the degree of research backing identified in the literature.

Interventions with a strong backing from research

Family and parenting interventions

There is good evidence that family and parenting interventions are effective in both preventing and reducing offending in young people (Chamberlain and Rosicky 1995; Farrington and Welsh 2002; Latimer 2001; Lipsey and Wilson 1998; Roberts and Camasso 1991; Woolfenden *et al.* 2002). Different types of family interventions were previously presented in this book, and will not be repeated here.

However, based on the offending literature, it is important to note that not all types of family and parenting programmes have been shown to produce desirable effects (Lipsey and Wilson 1998). For example, one review reports that the combination of school-based child training and parent training has been found to be promising in some studies and harmful in others (Farrington and Welsh 2002).

One review found that family and parenting interventions reduced recidivism by 21 per cent compared with other treatments or control. Stronger effects were found in: high risk cases; when the treatment targets the direct causes of offending behaviour; when behavioural–social learning approaches were used; and when models of service were matched to the learning styles of the clients (Dowden and Andrews 2003).

Wilderness challenge programmes

Wilderness challenge programmes involve young people participating in physically challenging activities, usually in an outdoor environment. Activities can include rock climbing and backpacking, although the programmes vary in terms of settings, types of activities and therapeutic goals (Gass 1993). Experimental education is a key aspect of wilderness programmes. Young people are involved in activities that challenge their skills and self-concepts, and are based on two dimensions of experimental learning:

- Building self-confidence, self-esteem and internalised locus of control through the mastery of a series of challenging physical activities. It is assumed that the new skills the young person obtains will empower the person, thereby reducing the likelihood that they will continue to behave in the same pattern of inappropriate or illegal behaviours.

- To solve challenging physical activities, positive group interactions and cooperation need to be employed to be successful. The young person will therefore learn prosocial and interpersonal skills by being involved in the activities and these skills can then be transferred to other situations.

A meta-analysis of wilderness challenge programmes by Wilson and Lipsey (2000) included 28 studies and 3000 young people mostly between the ages of 13 and 15. Their study reported an overall mean effect size for delinquency outcomes at a modest 0.18 (n = 22), equivalent to a re-offending rate of 29 per cent for programme participants versus 37 per cent for comparison subjects. They also reported that the length of the programme was not related to outcome among short-term programmes (up to six weeks); however, extended programmes (over ten weeks) showed smaller effects overall.

The intensity of the physical activities and whether a distinct therapeutic component (i.e. individual counselling, family therapy and group sessions) was included were the most influential characteristics of any programme. Programmes with relatively intense activities (those that employed strenuous solo and group expeditions and other difficult physical activities) or with therapeutic enhancements were most effective in reducing delinquent behaviour at post-test. The review does not report whether these effects were maintained over time.

The review included both randomised controlled trials and comparison studies. One limitation is that the sample only included white boys already arrested and convicted of crime, hence the results cannot be generalised to non-Caucasians or girls. Note that studies on boot camp programmes were only included if they focused on group cooperation and interpersonal skills development as well as the wilderness challenge. A review of studies on military style boot camps did not find that such interventions reduced offending behaviour (Wilson, MacKenzie and Mitchell 2005).

Cognitive behaviour programmes

Programmes using cognitive behaviour techniques have been found to be more successful in reducing re-offending than programmes that do not use such approaches (Antonowicz and Ross 1994; Izzo and Ross 1990; Kurtz 2002; Lipsey et al. 2001; Lipsey and Wilson 1998; Redondo et al. 1999). None of these studies specified the further characteristics of successful programmes, apart from the cognitive behaviour elements.

Lipsey et al. (2001) carried out a meta-analysis of cognitive behaviour programmes to reduce re-offending, both for young offenders and adults.

They included evaluations of programmes that were 'directed toward changing offenders' distorted or dysfunctional cognitions or teaching new cognitive skills in areas where offenders have deficits'. The therapeutic techniques were defined as being 'specific, relatively structured learning experiences designed to affect such cognitive processes as interpreting social cues, reasoning about right and wrong behaviour and making decisions about appropriate behaviour'. They did not include programmes where the cognitive behaviour component was part of a wider intervention. The reviewed interventions typically lasted from 11 to 20 weeks, for a total of ten hours or less of average weekly contact time.

Although the pooled treatment effect from across the studies was statistically significant and favoured CBT treatment, the effect was not consistent across studies. This is indicated by the fact that the confidence intervals of 11 out of the 14 studies crossed zero with significant heterogeneity.

The authors found that demonstration trials set up by researchers achieved much better results than those carried out on an ongoing basis. It was therefore concluded that it is not known whether the effects found in such trials could be replicated in mainstream settings (Lipsey et al. 2001). Smaller sample sizes and short-term measures of recidivism also produced larger effect sizes. Positive effects were found for young offenders both in institutional settings and for those on probation or parole.

Another review showed that behaviour programmes were effective in reducing recidivism in serious juvenile offenders when treated in the community or in institutions (Lipsey and Wilson 1998). Both a cognitive and a behavioural element have been found to be necessary for the intervention to be successful (Antonowicz and Ross 1994).

It is important to recognise the plethora of approaches that fit within the broader category of 'CBT', and the fact that we know very little about which of these approaches are more likely to produce positive change in young people. Interpersonal skills training was found by one review to produce positive changes for serious juvenile offenders, and there was consistent evidence for this, both for young people treated in the community, and for those who were treated in young offender institutions (Lipsey and Wilson 1998). Another review found that stronger effects from CBT are seen in combination with parenting programmes (Fonagy et al. 2002).

Interventions with some backing from research

The interventions listed here were found to be effective by some reviews, but not identified across the literature as being effective in reducing offending behaviour.

After-school recreation programmes were found by one review to be promising in terms of reducing crime in areas immediately around the recreation centre; this was based on three individual studies. However, this was disputed by another, less rigorous, review (Poyner 1993) that was based on five individual studies.

The effects of community-based mentoring on offending are uncertain, but Welsh and Hoshi (2002) identified seven individual studies and concluded that it is a promising intervention in terms of reducing crime, even though negative findings have been reported (Roberts *et al.* 2004).

A meta-analysis by Lipsey and Wilson (1998) reviewed research on interventions for young offenders treated in the community. The analysis pooled results for 200 studies, mainly conducted in the US. They identified the following interventions for which there were mixed, but generally positive, research findings:

- multiple services where the young offender and his or her family are provided with a choice of different services (for example, mentoring, group counselling, vocational training), traditional youth work support, or intensive case management with support tailored to the young person's needs (Lipsey and Wilson 1998)

- restitution in combination with probation or parole

- employment-related interventions

- academic programmes

- advocacy/social casework

- family counselling

- group counselling.

The same review also looked at interventions for young offenders that have been institutionalised. For this population individual and group counselling were found to have mixed but generally positive effects on recidivism (Lipsey and Wilson 1998).

Harmful interventions and interventions of no effect

The research on the following interventions was found to produce the opposite effects of what they intended. The reviews concluded that these interventions increased, rather than reduced, re-offending:

- traditional responses by the youth justice system (Kurtz 2002) such as probation or parole in combination with reduced caseloads or early release (Lipsey and Wilson 1998)

- deterrence programmes and awareness programmes involving tours of prisons or prison experiences (Antonowicz and Ross 1994; Lipsey and Wilson 1998; Petrosino *et al.* 2004; Redondo *et al.* 1999)

- vocational programmes (Lipsey and Wilson 1998).

Some reviewed interventions found no effect in either direction. A review on curfews to reduce crime reported mixed results from ten studies (Adams 2003). Some studies found no effect from the introduction of curfew orders, some a positive and some a negative effect in the young people. When looking at significant changes, half of these reported a positive effect, whilst the other half reported negative effects on crime from this intervention. Positive effects from curfew orders were associated with these being delivered as part of a wider programme of interventions. Other interventions that showed no effect were as follows.

- Sociological models; however, the authors do not provide information on what kinds of approaches were used within these models (Antonowicz and Ross 1994).

- Psychodynamic models (Antonowicz and Ross 1994).

- Milieu therapy (Lipsey and Wilson 1998). This is a treatment that focuses on changing the social environment of the young person. The 'milieu' supports the young person in learning life skills such as problem solving. Milieu therapy is similar to a therapeutic community.

- Therapeutic community. The report was based on one randomised controlled trial carried out in the UK. Study subjects were 13–15-year-old boys. There was no difference in reconviction rates between the boys in the therapeutic community, those allocated to a conventional house, or those ineligible for community treatment and treated elsewhere (Lees, Manning and Rawlings 1999).

- Correctional boot camps, or boot-camp-like programmes such as shock incarceration, were not found to reduce re-offending rates in a recent Campbell review (Wilson *et al.* 2005). The review looked at programmes for both adult and juvenile offenders, but did not find any statistically significant effects for either group. The included boot-camp programmes differed from the wilderness challenge interventions reviewed by Wilson and Lipsey (2000) in that they were more oriented towards correctional treatment and physical training.

Conclusion

There is a vast literature on interventions for young offenders, and this chapter has looked at available systematic reviews. But in spite of this large pool of research, few programmes have been rigorously evaluated across studies and systematic reviews are needed to focus on specific programmes for specific populations. There is also a need for more follow-up research, to look at the long-term effects of programmes. Offending behaviour is difficult to change, and it is important to be aware that even the most successful programmes achieve modest results. At present we know little about whether effects are sustained over time.

As indicated here, some treatment characteristics occur across successful programmes. These include: cognitive behaviour therapy, focusing on more than one technique (multimodal programmes), and family and parenting interventions. As such, successful treatments for young offenders appear to have much in common with those identified for conduct disordered young people. Again, it is important to be aware that many programmes have been carried out in demonstration trials, and it may be that the effects are weakened when these are implemented in usual services. Finally, there is a strong need for intervention research to be carried out in the UK, as the current research base is dominated by US studies.

14 Summary of Key Issues

As conduct disorders are the most common problems being referred to child and adolescent mental health services, it is important to increase the implementation of effective intervention programmes. Clearly, more resources are needed in practice, to deliver services for this population. The focus for this review has been the research evidence. Our main finding is that little systematic research relevant to the UK is currently available to underpin good practice.

For practitioners interested in basing their practice on available evidence it can be frustrating to hear that 'more research is needed'. At the moment, treatment programmes have mainly been developed and researched in the US, and to date little evaluation has been conducted in the UK. Fortunately, this is changing. For example, Pote and colleagues (2003) have developed a manual for family therapy, suitable for outcome research (Pote *et al.* 2003). The national evaluation of multidimensional treatment foster care (MTFC) in England aims to use a randomised controlled design, and the 2006 Care Matters green paper called for UK-based research on the effectiveness of functional family therapy (Department for Education and Skills 2006a).

A number of issues highlighted in this review need to be considered for future research and practice. To date, the quality of this research is variable, as discussed throughout this report. Tables detailing the critical appraisal of key studies can be found on the FOCUS website at www.rcpsych.ac.uk/crtu/focus/focuspublications.aspx.

Key findings

Overall, programmes that target all factors in a young person's life (education, family issues, offending, peer relations) appear to be more effective than those focusing on one area. In many ways, the most promising approaches, such as functional family therapy and multidimensional foster care, represent extended versions of traditional social work, with strong links to education and mental health teams.

- Family therapy programmes offer the most promising research evidence to date. Studies looking at overall effects of these programmes indicate that they can improve behaviour in conduct disordered young people, and young offenders (Wolpert *et al.* 2006). Functional family therapy is one of the most promising amongst these interventions. Careful evaluation of multisystemic therapy (MST) did not find that this intervention was more effective than 'treatment as usual'. On the other hand, the researchers also did not find any harmful effects resulting from MST (Littell 2005). MST is one of the most extensively researched programmes to date, and similar practice-based research is needed before we know which programmes are most likely to improve behaviour, for which young people. Research indicates that parent training programmes are effective for younger children, but not for conduct disordered adolescents (Wolpert *et al.* 2006).

- A promising intervention for young people placed outside of the family home is multidimensional treatment foster care (Wolpert *et al.* 2006). The aim of this comprehensive intervention is to return the young person to their local community. This particular type of foster care is currently being rolled out in England, and an evaluation is planned alongside practice. A forthcoming Cochrane review will look at the effectiveness of treatment foster care (Turner and Macdonald 2006).

- The research evidence is inconclusive as to the effect of programmes that teach young people social and problem-solving skills, or anger management. There are myriad individual treatment programmes available, but few of these have been rigorously researched. Furthermore, there is a lack of details on how programmes are delivered, and the treatment content. Most of these programmes use principles of cognitive behaviour therapy (CBT), an approach that has also been found effective in reducing juvenile re-offending (Lipsey et al. 2001). One review found some negative effects from social skills training programmes (Kavale et al. 1997).

- The research evidence to date does not support the use of medication to treat aggression in conduct disordered young people (Wolpert et al. 2006). There is a lack of double-blind placebo-controlled studies, and potential side effects are severe. There are also ethical implications associated with medication, and long-term effects need to be considered carefully.

- Few studies have looked at the effect on interventions specifically for young people involved in firesetting and arson.

- There is increasing interest in the role that diet, or vitamin supplements, can play in managing difficult behaviour. Research in this field is promising, but still in its pilot phase (Gesch et al. 2002; Kaplan et al. 2004; Liu et al. 2004). No intervention trials were found that fulfilled our inclusion criteria.

- This review has also considered treatments for young offenders. Findings for this population largely mirror those for conduct disordered young people. Family and parenting interventions are the most promising programmes. Wilderness challenge projects have also been found to be effective in reducing re-offending, but it is not clear from the literature whether this is an intervention likely to work for young people with conduct disorder (Wilson and Lipsey 2000). Deterrence programmes for young offenders have been shown to increase, rather than decrease, offending behaviour (Petrosino et al. 2004).

- Overall, treatments appear to be more effective when they directly impact on young people's problem behaviour, by limiting social interaction with delinquent peers, supporting the development of social skills, increasing supervision and using techniques such as behaviour contracting to encourage prosocial activities.

Limitations of current research

- Most research to date has been carried out with male participants. Conduct disorders are increasing in girls (Green *et al.* 2005), and more research is needed to establish what works for this population. Studies of MTFC indicate that special considerations are needed in relation to girls that are involved in offending (Shepard and Chamberlain 2005).

- There is also a lack of research on particular sub-groups within the conduct disordered population, for example sex offenders and firesetters. Similarly, studies to date do not tend to specify whether the participants suffered from a particular type of conduct disorder (socialised or unsocialised).

- More follow-up studies are needed to ascertain whether improved behaviour is maintained over time. In particular, studies need to examine the relationship between the initial severity of the problems or the duration of the programme, and the maintenance of effects over time.

- More research is needed to test the effectiveness of programmes in clinical practice as opposed to trials conducted in universities with volunteer families.

- More information is needed on the cost effectiveness of all types of intervention and how to decide the optimum mix of programmes. Some of the most promising programmes are also the most expensive.

Appendix 1: Diagnostic Criteria for Conduct Disorder

ICD-10 (WHO 1994)

A repetitive and persistent pattern of behaviour, in which either the basic rights of others or major age-appropriate societal norms or rules are violated, lasting at least six months, during which the individual presents with some of the following symptoms (see individual subcategories for rules or numbers of symptoms):

1. unusually frequent or severe temper tantrums for his or her developmental level

2. often argues with adults

3. often actively refuses adults' requests or defies rules

4. often, apparently deliberately, does things that annoy other people

5. often blames others for own mistakes or misbehaviour

6. often touchy or easily annoyed by others

7. often angry or resentful

8. often spiteful or vindictive

9. frequent and marked lying (except to avoid abusive treatment)

10. excessive fighting with others, with frequent initiations of fights (not siblings)

11. uses a weapon that can cause serious physical harm to others

12. often stays out after dark without permission (beginning the age of 13)

13. physical cruelty to other people (e.g. ties up, cuts, or burns a victim)

14. physical cruelty to animals

15. deliberate destruction of others' property (other than by firesetting)

16. deliberate firesetting with a risk or intention of causing serious damage

17. at least two episodes of stealing of objects of value from home (excluding food)

18. at least two episodes of stealing outside the home without confronting the victim (e.g. shoplifting, burglary, forgery)

19. frequent truancy from school beginning before 13 years of age

20. running away from home (unless this was to avoid physical or sexual abuse)

21. any episode of crime involving confrontation with the victim

22. forcing another person into sexual activity against their wishes

23. frequent bullying of others (e.g. deliberate infliction of pain or hurt, including persistent intimidation, tormenting, or molestation)

24. breaks into someone else's house, building, or car.

Symptoms in 11, 13, 15, 16, 20, 21, and 23 need only have occurred once for the criterion to be fulfilled.

If criteria are met for dissocial personality, schizophrenia, manic episode, depressive episode, pervasive developmental disorders or hyperkinetic disorder these diagnoses will take precedence over conduct disorder. If the criteria are met for emotional disorder the diagnosis should be mixed disorder of conduct and emotions.

It is recommended to note whether the onset is in childhood (before the age of ten years) or in adolescence. It is recommended that the levels of hyperactivity, emotional disturbance, and severity of the conduct disorder are considered.

Key sub-types are: conduct disorder confined to the family context; unsocialised conduct disorder; socialised conduct disorder oppositional defiant disorders; other conduct disorders; conduct disorder unspecified. Each of these are identified by a different range of behaviours from the above list.

DSM-IV (APA 1994)

A. A repetitive and persistent pattern of behaviour in which the basic rights of others or major age-appropriate societal norms or rules are violated, as manifested by the presence of three (or more) of the following criteria in the past 12 months, with at least one criterion present in the past six months:

Aggression to people and animals:

1. often bullies, threatens or intimidates others

2. often initiates physical fights

3. has used weapon that could cause physical harm

4. has been physically cruel to people

5. has been physically cruel to animals

6. has stolen while confronting the victim (e.g. mugging)

7. has forced someone into sexual activity.

Destruction of property:

1. has deliberately engaged in firesetting

2. has deliberately destroyed others' property (not by firesetting).

Deceitfulness or theft:

1. has broken into someone else's house, building, or car

2. often lies to obtain goods or favours or to avoid obligations

3. has stolen items of non-trivial value without confronting a victim.

Serious violations of rules:

1. often stays out at night despite parental prohibition, beginning before the age of 13 years

2. has run away from home overnight at least twice (or once without returning)

3. is often truant from school, beginning before the age of 13 years.

B. The disturbance in behaviour causes clinically significant impairment in social, academic or occupational functioning.

C. If the individual is aged 18 years or older, and criteria are not met for Antisocial Personality Disorder.

Code based on age at onset:

- 312.81 Conduct Disorder, Childhood-Onset Type: onset of at least one criterion characteristic of Conduct Disorder prior to age ten years.

- 312.82 Conduct Disorder, Adolescent-Onset Type: absence of any criteria characteristic of Conduct Disorder prior to age ten years.

- 312.89 Conduct Disorder, Unspecified Onset: age at onset is not known.

Specify severity:

- *Mild:* few if any conduct problems in excess of those required to make the diagnosis and conduct problems that cause only minor harm to others.

- *Moderate:* number of conduct problems and effect on others intermediate between mild and severe.

- *Severe:* many conduct problems in excess of those required to make the diagnosis or conduct problems cause considerable harm to others.

Appendix 2: Useful Terms for Understanding and Assessing Research

This glossary has been adapted from www.whatworksforchildren.org.uk/glossary.htm and explains different types of study design and some key concepts in systematic reviewing.[1]

When reading a research report it is essential to think about its quality and any possible bias in the study. This may result from systematic errors in the way the study was designed or in the analysis of data. Some typical factors that may result in bias are:

- the wording of a question asked (which may encourage a particular response)

- the way the assessment was carried out – scores may be affected if the interviewers know which treatment condition each participant received

- the selection of people to be studied – is the sample truly representative of the population about whom claims are being made? For example, does a study purporting to be about conduct disordered young people only include young people with non-clinical behaviour problems?

Critical appraisal is a technique for reading research and working out how valid and relevant the research is. Critical appraisal helps us to work out how likely it is that the results of research are biased because of the way the research was carried out.

In studies of interventions (services or activities) a study may conclude that an intervention was effective in dealing with a problem. Critical appraisal can help us work out if the intervention only *appeared* to be effective because of bias in the research methods. This may happen, for example, if:

- no comparison group was used and those receiving the intervention would have got better anyway

- all the people who did not like the intervention left the study and their results were not included

- the young people in the comparison group were very different to the group given the intervention.

The following research terms are arranged alphabetically. Words underlined are explained in other sections of the glossary.

Case study

A case study is used when the researcher wants to investigate the complexities of a single case and its interaction with the surroundings. A case study needs to be described in detail so that the reader may relate the findings to a similar case.

Example of case-control study: what are the risk factors for suicide in adolescence?

A group of 40 young people aged 15–18 with one suicide attempt (or more) are matched with another similar sized group of 15–18-year-olds who do not have a record of attempted suicide. The matching ensures that the social and economic environment of the groups is similar (e.g. urban, school drop-outs, single-parent families). The researchers will have various theories about risk factors (what is causing the suicide attempts). For example, one risk factor could be a poor relationship with the parents. The researchers would look at whether there was a difference in this between the two groups. Similarly, they could look at other factors such as relationships outside the family, involvement in work, peer relationships, hobbies, etc.

Case-control studies

Individuals with a particular problem are 'matched' with people (the *control group*) without the problem. The exposure of the two groups to possible causes is then compared. This can be used to investigate risk factors.

Cohort studies

These collect information from or about children at regular intervals, often from shortly after birth until later in adulthood. Cohort studies can be used to investigate associations between early development and experiences, and later outcomes. For example, a cohort study may ask 'What distinguishes those people who are able to move out of poverty?'

A limitation of both case-control and cohort studies is that there may be other factors not measured which are responsible for the differences in outcomes between the groups in the study. For example, if we compare high accident families with low accident families to identify risk factors of home injury, we will be in danger of overlooking things. We might not realise that in one area the health visitors are running an accident awareness campaign, or local stores do not stock a certain type of safety equipment.

Confidence interval (CI)

A confidence interval associated with a result tells us the likelihood that the same result would be found if the whole population were studied rather than just a sample. For example, a newspaper might report that the average IQ of researchers is 99. If the 95 per cent confidence interval is 80–120 this means that we can be 95 per cent sure that the average IQ of all researchers of the type sampled will be between 80 and 120.

A measure of effect tells us something about what the intervention does for a particular sample. For example, one research study found that family and parenting programmes decreased the time spent by delinquent young people in institutions by an average of 51.34 days. The 95 per cent confidence interval was 30.16 to 72.52 days. This means that we can be 95 per cent certain that, when delivered to the wider population of delinquent young people, these types of family and parenting programmes will reduce the time spent in institutions by between 30.16 and 72.52 days.

If we are examining the confidence interval around a mean difference (i.e. the difference between average results for the intervention group and the control group), and the interval includes the value zero, the relationship between the intervention and the outcome is not statistically significant as it includes the possibility that there is zero effect.

We should examine confidence intervals carefully, because this lack of statistical significance may be because the sample is small, rather than because the treatment is not effective (in which case there will usually be a large confidence interval). Equally in a very large sample a very small and possibly unimportant effect may be statistically significant.

Control group

A control group is used in order to try to establish whether any effect found in the intervention group was due to the intervention or would have occurred anyway. The *control group* is the comparison group that gets a different service/intervention (or no service/intervention) from the intervention group.

Critical appraisal

A systematic way of assessing a research study, and considering it in terms of validity, bias, results and relevance to your own work.

Effect size

The effect size (d) or standardised mean difference (SMD) is a way of quantifying the difference between two groups, when one group has had an experimental treatment and the other has not (the control group). The 'd' statistic of effect size is calculated by subtracting the mean of the control group from the mean of the treatment group and dividing by their common standard deviation. In meta-analysis the effect sizes from individual trials are combined and each d is weighted according to pre-set study quality criteria. Conventionally, effect sizes of $d = 0.2$ are considered small, $d = 0.5$ medium, and $d = 0.8$ large. Some behaviours are particularly difficult to change, and some outcomes have a wider application than others. It can therefore be argued that for certain outcomes, such as violent criminal behaviour, even a small effect size has practical significance (Gottfredson *et al.* 2002; Lipsey 1992).

The effect size should be viewed in relation to the *confidence interval.*

Effectiveness

Describes the extent to which an intervention improves the outcome(s) for those receiving it and the extent to which these benefits outweigh the harm (if any) caused by the intervention.

Heterogeneity

In meta-analyses tests are carried out to measure whether the treatment effect is consistent across the included studies. This is called a test for heterogeneity. Although some variability in results is expected by chance, it may not be reasonable to pool findings if the results vary considerably due to differences in participants, clinical setting or treatment protocols.

Intervention

A type of service, programme or policy (e.g. health promotion campaigns) or (in medicine) a drug, device or other treatments.

Intervention group

The group that receives an intervention (service, medicine, treatment). See also *case-control studies,* and *randomised controlled trials.*

Meta-analysis

A statistical technique that pools the results from several studies into one overall estimate of the effect of an intervention. See also *systematic review.*

Odds

Odds give a ratio of occurrence to non-occurrence of an event. Odds are a way of expressing the likelihood of an event such as reconviction after an intervention. The odds of reconviction would be the expected number of young offenders reconvicted divided by the expected number of young offenders not reconvicted. If three out of every ten young offenders receiving the intervention are reconvicted the odds would be $3/7 = 0.4$ (see further explanation below under *odds ratio*).

Odds ratio (OR)

The odds ratio (OR) looks at the relationship between the effect in the control versus the intervention group. It is the ratio of the odds of the event occurring in the experimental group relative to the odds of the event occurring in the *control group.* This is sometimes used as a measure of the effectiveness of an intervention. The OR is calculated by dividing the odds of the event occurring in the intervention group by the odds of it occurring in the control group.

Example: What effect do parenting programmes have on reconviction? (NB: this is a fictional example)

In the intervention group, parents of 32 young people received a parenting programme. In the control group parents of 30 young people did not.

	Parenting programme	Control
Reconvicted	2	20

Odds that those whose parents receive parenting programmes are reconvicted: $2/30 = 0.07$.
Odds that those whose parents do not receive parenting programmes are reconvicted: $20/10 = 2$.
Odds ratio: $0.07/2 = 0.035$.

If the event is a negative event, such as reconviction and the OR < 1, then the treatment may be effective. In the example above, OR = 0.035, which means that parenting programmes could have an effect on reconvictions.

If OR = 1 the intervention has no effect (i.e. no difference between the intervention and the control group). An OR < 1 would suggest that the treatment of interest was actually less effective than no treatment (or an alternative). On its own, an OR is not very informative – a *confidence interval* is also needed (see above).

Outcome

Changes or effects that happen as a result of the intervention. Outcomes may be for: individuals, families, communities or organisations. For example, a reduction in offending behaviour may be an outcome of an (effective) offending prevention programme.

P-value

A p-value expresses the likelihood that a result was due to chance. For example, p = .03 means that there is a 3 per cent chance that the population value lies outside the *confidence interval*.

Population

In statistical terms, the population is the complete set of whatever is the object of study (individuals, objects or scores), from which a sample may be taken in order to make inferences about the whole population.

Power

The probability that an experiment will be able to detect an effect of a variable (for example an intervention) if the variable has a true effect.

Quasi-experimental studies

Used to examine the effects of an intervention. One or more control groups are used but participants are not randomly allocated to one group or the other. 'Naturally occurring' control groups are often used. Commonly, one group will receive a particular service while the other does not, or receives another type of service. In a quasi-experimental study the two groups are sometimes matched on key characteristics. However, it is not possible to match on all relevant factors including unknown ones. It may be that the service is delivered to the group that needs it the most, enhancing the risk of bias as the two groups are not truly comparable.

Practical reasons will sometimes require a quasi-experimental design. When evaluating the impact from changes to the environment such as school-wide violence prevention programmes, an area-wide implementation is necessary. In these cases you can only compare one area with another because it is impossible to randomly decide who will receive the intervention within one area.

Example: Does social skills training improve behaviour?

One group receives social skills training; the other does not. There is a risk that the extent of young people's problem behaviour will influence the allocation of service. If those who have lower levels of behaviour problems are enrolled in the groups because they are perceived to be easier to work with, and then compared with a group with more serious problems, our findings will be biased.

Randomised controlled trials (RCT)

An experiment in which individuals are randomly allocated either to receive or not receive an intervention (or to receive a different intervention). The groups are then followed up to determine the effect of the intervention, by identifying differences between those who did and those who did not receive it.

Example: What is more effective in reducing offending behaviour in young people – parenting programmes or curfew orders?

The amount of offending behaviour is measured at baseline (police records, parent- and self-report, school records) for all young people. All the families agreeing to participate in the study are then randomly allocated to receive curfew orders or attend parenting groups or be on a waiting list (control group). Twelve months later the offending behaviour is again measured and the groups compared. Preferably, further measures are taken one, two or more years later to measure long-term effects.

Reliability

Refers to the likelihood that the same results would be found if the study was repeated in the same way elsewhere.

Sample

A subset of cases (individuals, objects or scores) selected from the population of interest.

Sample size and power

A rigorous study involves some consideration of sample size – or the number of participants to recruit to the study. This is a crucial determinant of whether a difference will be detected if it really exists. Sometimes the number of participants in a study is chosen because the number 'seems appropriate', or because of a limited study budget. However, the appropriate size for a particular study depends on the likely size of the effect you are trying to detect – for example, the likely size of the *odds ratio* (OR), or the magnitude of the difference between two means. Where the effect is likely to be small, then larger study numbers are required in order to detect the effect.

Standardised mean difference (SMD)

See definition for *effect size.*

Statistical significance (see p-value)

Significance levels show you how likely it is that a result is due to chance. The level at which a result is said to be 'significant' is arbitrary but the most common level used is .05. If a result is said to be significant at the .05 level ($p > .05$) this means that the finding has a 5 per cent (.05) chance of not being true (see also *p-value*). A statistically significant result does not necessarily mean that a result is significant in a practical sense. For example, a very small and unimportant effect may be found to be statistically significant if a very large sample was studied.

Systematic review

A systematic review (SR) is a critical assessment and evaluation of existing research that addresses a specific question by following a fixed approach for locating, appraising and analysing all studies addressing the question of interest. SRs can be used to look at the effectiveness of interventions (for example, do wilderness challenge programmes for young offenders reduce their likelihood of re-offending?). When a systematic review pools data across studies to provide an estimate of the overall treatment effect, we call it a *meta-analysis.*

Note

1   What Works for Children? was funded by the Economic and Social Research Council and spent four years looking at what helps and hinders the use of research evidence in health and social care practice (www.whatworksforchildren.org.uk).

Appendix 3: Search Strategy

Identifying the research evidence

To identify papers evaluating interventions to treat conduct disorder, searches were conducted on MEDLINE, PsychINFO, EMBASE Psychiatry, Cochrane Library, Database of Abstracts of Reviews of Effects (DARE), American College of Physicians (ACP) Journal Club, British Nursing Index, and Cumulative Index to Nursing and Allied Health Literature (CINAHL) databases for papers published between 1980 and April 2006. The same databases were searched to identify studies on pharmaceutical interventions published between 1999 and 2005, to look for studies published after the systematic review by Fonagy and colleagues (2002).

To identify papers on interventions to reduce youth offending, searches were conducted on MEDLINE, Australian Educational Index (AEI), British Educational Index (BEI), C2-RIPE (Campbell Collaboration Register for Reviews of Interventions and Policy Evaluation), C2-SPECTR (Campbell Collaboration Social, Psychological, Education and Criminological Trials Registry), ChildData, CINAHL, Cochrane Library, Criminal Justice Abstracts, EMBASE Psychiatry, ERIC, HMIC (Health Management Information Consortium), and PsychINFO databases for papers published between 1990 and October 2004.

The search terms in Table A3.1 were sought in a record's title, abstract, full text, key word, caption text, MESH headings, keyword and heading words, ISSN (TOC), drug manufacturer name, name of substance word, table of contents, and identifiers.

For studies to be included in this book the following inclusion criteria were applied:

- Subjects were on average over the age of ten, with conduct disorder or had been involved with the juvenile justice system for their antisocial behaviour.

- Subjects were on average under the age of 18, with conduct disorder or had been involved with the juvenile justice system for their antisocial behaviour.

- A conduct disorder diagnosis was not required when including studies on school-based intervention.

- The studies included some form of intervention intended to reduce antisocial or aggressive behaviours.

- The minimum number of subjects included in the studies was 30 unless the study was a crossover design.

- The studies were in English.

Studies were excluded if:

- the majority of young people did not have a conduct disorder diagnosis or were not involved in the juvenile justice system for their antisocial behaviour

- the majority of young people had learning difficulties, as measured by IQ 80

- the main target of the treatment was sex offences.

All relevant studies were critically appraised as described in Appendix 4.

Table A3.1: Search terms used to identify papers		
Conduct disorder interventions	**Pharmaceutical interventions**	**Interventions for young offenders**
Search terms used to identify controlled trials, systematic reviews and meta-analyses	Limited search on the most well-known pharmaceutical agents used in treatment	Search terms used to identify systematic reviews and meta-analyses
conduct disorder*	stimulant*	juvenile delinq*
behaviour* problem*	methylphenidate	disordered offend*
behavior* problem*	lithium	juvenile offend*
anti-social personality disorder*	clonidine	youth offend*
antisocial personality disorder*	anticonvulsant*	young offend*
anti-social behaviour*	carbamazepine buspirone	
anti-social behavior*	beta*	
antisocial behaviour*	clozapine	
antisocial behavior*	risperidone	
oppositional defiant	neuroleptic*	
aggressi*	pharma*	
violen*	sodium AND valproate	
fire*		
pyro*		
fight*		
bull*		

Table A3.1 cont.

Conduct disorder interventions	Pharmaceutical interventions	Interventions for young offenders
Search terms used to identify controlled trials, systematic reviews and meta-analyses	Limited search on the most well-known pharmaceutical agents used in treatment	Search terms used to identify systematic reviews and meta-analyses
child*	child*	child*
adolesc*	adolesc*	adolesc*
juven*	juven*	juven*
young pe*	young pe*	young pe*
youth*	youth*	youth*
teen-age*	teen-age*	teen-age*
teenage*	teenage*	teenage*
teen age*	teen age*	teen age*

* Trunction, which means that the search included all words starting with spelling before.

Appendix 4: Critical Appraisal

Evidence-based practice is not simply research-informed practice. Because research varies in quality and relevance, it needs to be assessed before it is used to inform clinical decision-making. A hierarchy of evidence is often used as a rule of thumb. Within the hierarchy framework, the best evidence comes from systematic reviews and meta-analyses, the second best from individual randomised controlled trials, followed by cohort studies, case-control studies, cross-sectional surveys and case reports. The hierarchy framework has been contested because a study's methods also need to fit with the question asked. A randomised controlled trial is usually, but not always, the most appropriate way of evaluating the *effectiveness* of an intervention. If the question is concerned with other aspects of service delivery, such as children and young people's experiences, then qualitative research methods may be more appropriate (Petticrew and Roberts 2006).

Each intervention study included in this book has been critically appraised according to pre-set criteria. The critical appraisals of included reviews and trials are not presented here, but are available on www.rcpsych.ac.uk. Boxes A4.1 and A.4.2 show the two types of critical appraisal tools used in this review.

Box A4.1 Completed critical appraisal tool for the systematic review carried out by Mytton *et al.* (2006)

Author/s:
Mytton, J. A., DiGuiseppi, C., Gough, D. A., Taylor, R. S. and Logan, S.

Title:
'School based secondary prevention programms for preventing violence.'

Source and date:
Cochrane Library, 2006.

Focus of the paper

Design:
Systematic review and meta-analysis of randomised controlled trials.

Population:

Children in mandatory education, identified as being aggressive, or at risk of being aggressive.

Are the results valid?

Is the question clearly focused?

Clearly focused question stating that this is a systematic review of randomised controlled trials of secondary school-based violence prevention programmes.

Is the search thorough?

The search covered all the main databases: Cochrane Library, MedLine, Embase, National Research Register, PsycLIT, PsycInfo, ERIC, CINAHL, Dissertation Abstracts, IBSS, Social Sciences Index, NCJRS, Campbell Library.

Bibliographies of published reviews and trials. Handsearch in the journal Aggression and Violent Behaviour (1996-98).

Contacted international organisations and experts, and authors of all relevant studies to identify unpublished reports.

A comprehensive search up to and including 2001. Three further databases were searched in 2003. It is unfortunate that the 2003 search was not a complete update.

• *Inclusion criteria:*

Randomised controlled trials.

Interventions in primary and secondary education.

• *Exclusion criteria:*

Interventions that target related behaviours such as youth offending, antisocial behaviour, disruptive behaviour without also targeting aggression or violent behaviour.

Interventions to promote positive behaviours, unless their aim clearly stated reduction in aggression and/or violence.

Interventions where the main element was delivered outside of school.

Is the validity of included studies adequately assessed?

The quality assessment of relevant studies was thorough and encompassed the following steps:

Search hits were screened by two authors, and studies were excluded based on title, abstract and key words.

Full text reports of potentially eligible studies were read by two authors, who extracted data according to study eligibility, study participants, intervention, follow-up, outcomes.

Study quality was assessed according to their method of group assignment, allocation concealment, blinding of outcome assessment and loss to follow-up.

Authors were contacted for missing data.

Differences were resolved by discussion.

Placebo groups were preferred over non-intervention control groups. The analysis used the intent-to-treat principle.

Cluster randomised trials were adjusted for.

Details of individual studies

How many individual studies were included?

Fifty-six eligible trials were identified; 36 of these were suitable for inclusion in the meta-analysis.

In what countries were the treatment studies conducted?

Not stated.

If medication was used, what were the dosages of medication used for each study?

Not applicable.

Are the studies focused on boys or girls or both?

The majority of samples were boys; 22 out of 34 studies included both girls and boys; 12 studies looked at boys only.

What are the results?

How big is the overall effect?

Overall reduction in aggressive behaviour: standardised mean difference (SMD) = 0.41 (95% confidence interval 0.56 to 0.26).

This effect was maintained in the studies that reported outcomes at 12-month follow-up SMD = 0.40 (95% CI 0.73 to 0.06).

Effects by type of treatment programme:

Teaching relationship and social skills: SMD = –0.61 (–0.87 to –0.35).

Teaching problem-solving skills and anger control: SMD = (–0.39) –0.61 to –0.16), but with significant heterogeneity.

A mix of the two types of interventions: SMD = –0.28 (–0.55 to –0.01), with moderate hetrogeneity.

Effects appeared similar in primary and secondary schools.

Are the results consistent from study to study?

Tests for heterogeneity identified wide variations among studies in terms of the interventions' effects. This is seen in some of the confidence intervals above.

If the results of the review have been combined, was it reasonable to do so?

The authors were cautious in combining the effects. Evidence of heterogeneity suggested that a random-effects model was appropriate. A fixed-effects model was run as a sensitivity analysis.

How precise are the results?

The overall finding at post-test is relatively precise: 95 per cent confidence interval 0.56 to 0.26.

The result at follow-up was less precise: 95 per cent confidence interval 0.73 to 0.06.

Interpretation of the results – will they help in making decisions about patients?

Do conclusions flow from evidence that is reviewed?

Conclusions flow from the evidence presented, which is that school-based secondary prevention programmes are effective in reducing violence in the short term (up to one year). The authors pay attention to weaknesses in the studies, most notably the lack of blinded allocation and assessment, and poor reporting.

Are sub-group analyses interpreted cautiously?

Sub-group analyses were specified in advance. Most sub-group analyses contained more than ten studies, apart from 'type of intervention'.

Can the conclusions and data be generalised to other settings?

The findings from this review are promising and relevant for school psychologists, social workers and teachers. However, more information would have been useful on the types of interventions and characteristics of the children.

Were all important outcomes considered?

This review is focused on aggression. Although relevant outcomes such as juvenile delinquency appear to have been excluded, it is useful that the review focused on one particular outcome.

Are the benefits worth the harms and the costs?

No negative outcomes were reported. Although the long-term effects of some programmes appeared to be statistically non-significant, school-based violence prevention programmes appear to be effective.

Box A4.2 Completed critical appraisal tool for the randomised controlled trial by Rhode et al. 2004

Author/s:
Rhode, P., Clarke, G. N., Mace, D. E., Jorgensen, J. S. and Seeley, J. R.

Title of paper:
'An efficacy/effectiveness study of cognitive-behavioral treatment for adolescents with comorbid major depression and conduct disorder.'

Source and date:
Journal of American Academy of Child and Adolescent Psychiatry (2004) 43, 6, 660–668.

Are the results of this trial valid?

Are you using the right research paper to answer your particular question?

This study evaluates the effectiveness of a cognitive-behavioural group intervention, the Adolescent Coping With Depression (CWD-A) course, for depressed adolescents with comorbid conduct disorder. In this trial CWD-A is compared with a programme focusing on life skill/tutoring (LS).

Intervention(s):

CWD-A is a group intervention that combines cognitive and behavioural strategies. Participants are taught mood monitoring, how to improve social skills, increase pleasant activities, decrease anxiety, reduce depressogenic cognitions, improve communication, conflict resolution, and relapse prevention. The training also targets reading and writing, and includes a reward system for attendance.

LS includes reviews of current events, life skills training and academic tutoring. It aims to educate participants on basic life skills in a supportive and non-judgemental manner.

Was the group of patients clearly defined?

- *Population:*

Ninety-three young people with comorbid conduct disorder (CD) and major depressive disorder (MDD) according to DSM-IV criteria, aged 13–17, all able to converse in English. Exclusion criteria were: charges of first-degree assault (intent to seriously kill or severely harm another person), psychotic symptoms.

- *Outcomes:*

Depression: interviewers completed a 17-item version of the Hamilton Depression Rating Scale; adolescents completed the Beck Depression Inventory-II.
Conduct disorder: assessed by the Child Behavior Checklist (CBCL).
Psychosocial functioning: interviewers used the 100-point Children's Global Adjustment Scale; adolescents completed the Social Adjustment Scale–Self-Report for Youth (23 items).

Participants were assessed post-treatment and at 6-and 12-month follow-up interviews.

Was the assignment of patients to treatments randomised?

Ninety-three young people were randomly assigned to either the CWD-A course (n = 45) or LS (n = 48). Randomisation occurred within cohort using a random numbers table. There were nine cohorts in all.

Were all patients who entered the trial accounted for at its conclusion?

A flow chart is presented, clearly showing drop-outs at each assessment time point.

An intention-to-treat analysis was conducted and compared with an analysis including data available at follow-up only. The two approaches yielded an identical pattern of results, probably because attrition was very low (6% at 12-month follow-up). Only results based on the follow-up sample are presented in the article.

Were they analysed in the groups to which they were randomised?
Yes.

Were patients and clinicians kept 'blind' to which treatment was being received?
Due to the nature of the intervention, complete blinding was not possible. Interviewers who carried out the assessment of participants were blinded, and did not know which treatment participants had received.

Aside from the experimental treatment, were the groups treated equally?
The two treatment groups did not differ on use of mental health treatment other than the research interventions.

What are the results?

How large was the treatment effect?
Major depressive disorder recovery rates were significantly higher in the CWD-A condition (17 young people out of 44 recovered, 39%) than in the LS group (9 out of 47, 19%). OR = 2.66 (95% confidence interval 1.03 to 6.85). These differences were not found at 6- and 12- month follow-up.

Conduct disorder recovery rates did not differ significantly between the two treatment groups: CWD-A (4 out of 44, 9%), LS (8 out of 47, 17%), OR = 0.49 (95% CI 0.14 to 1.75). There were no significant differences in conduct disorder recovery rates at 6-and 12-month follow-up.

No significant effects were found at 6- and 12-month follow-up on: suicide attempts, substance abuse/dependence, ADHD, anxiety disorders, residential treatment, outpatient treatment, medications, number of arrests.

No significant effects were found in respect to gender.

How precise is the estimate of treatment effect?
The CI for MDD recovery rates was wide (1.03–6.85) at post-test, and not significant at follow-up.

What are the implications of this paper for local practice?

Are the results of this study generalisable to your patient?
These are key questions to consider when deciding whether research findings are relevant to local policy and practice.

Does your patient resemble those in the study?

Are there alternative treatments available?

Appendix 5: Resources

CAMHS Evidence Based Practice Unit
Sub-Department of Clinical Health Psychology
University College London
Gower Street
London WC1E 6BT
www.ucl.ac.uk/clinical-health-psychology/Pages/camhs.htm

Child and Adolescent Mental Health Service Mapping
www.camhsmapping.org.uk

Centre for Evidence-Based Mental Health
Department of Psychiatry
University of Oxford
Warneford Hospital
Oxford OX3 7JX
01865 266476
www.cebmh.com

Centre for Reviews and Dissemination
University of York
York YO10 5DD
01904 321040
www.york.ac.uk/inst/crd

Every Child Matters: Change for Children
www.everychildmatters.gov.uk
www.everychildmatters.gov.uk/health/camhs/

Mental Health Foundation
83 Victoria Street
London SW1H 0HW
020 7802 0300
www.mentalhealth.org.uk

MIND (National Association for Mental Health)
Granta House
15–19 Broadway
London E15 4BQ
020 8519 2122
www.mind.org.uk

National Children's Bureau
8 Wakely Street
London EC1V 7QE
020 7843 6000
www.ncb.org.uk

National Family and Parenting Institute
430 Highgate Studios
53–79 Highgate Road
London NW5 1TL
020 7424 3460
www.familyandparenting.org

National Service Framework for Children, Young People and Maternity Services
www.dh.gov.uk/PolicyAndGuidance/HealthAndSocialCareTopics/ChildrenServices/
ChildrenServicesInformation/fs/en

Research in Practice
Blacklers Park Road
Dartington Hall
Totnes TQ9 6EQ
01803 868816
www.rip.org.uk

YoungMinds
102–108 Clerkenwell Road
London EC1M 5SA
020 7336 8445
www.youngminds.org.uk

Youth Justice Board
www.yjb.gov.uk

References

Achenbach, T. M. and Edelbrock, C. (1991) *Manual for the Child Behavior Checklist and Revised Child Behaviour Profile.* Burlington, VT: University Associates in Psychiatry.

Adams, K. (2003) 'The effectiveness of juvenile curfews at crime prevention.' *Annals of the American Academy of Political and Social Science 587,* 136–159.

Adler, R., Nunn, R., Northam, E., Lebnan, V. and Ross, R. (1994) 'Secondary prevention of childhood firesetting.' *Journal of the American Academy of Child and Adolescent Psychiatry 33,* 8, 1194–1202.

Alessi, N. E. and Magen, J. (1988) 'Comorbidity of other psychiatric disturbances in depressed, psychiatrically hospitalized children.' *American Journal of Psychiatry 145,* 1582–1584.

Alexander, J. F., Barton, C., Schiavo, R. S. and Parsons, B. V. (1976) 'Systems-behavioral intervention with families of delinquents: therapist characteristics, family behavior, and outcome.' *Journal of Consulting and Clinical Psychology 44,* 656–664.

Alexander, J. F. and Parsons, B. V. (1973) 'Short-term behavioral intervention with delinquent families: impact on family process and recidivism.' *Journal of Abnormal Psychology 81,* 3, 219–225.

American Academy of Child and Adolescent Psychiatry (1997) 'Practice parameters for the assessment and treatment of children and adolescents with conduct disorder.' *Journal of American Academy of Child and Adolescent Psychiatry 36,* 122–139.

Andrews, D. A., Zinger, I., Hoge, R. D., Bonta, J., Gendreau, P. and Cullen, F. T. (1990) 'Does correctional treatment work? A clinically relevant and psychologically informed meta-analysis.' *Criminology 28,* 3, 369–404.

Angold, A. and Costello, E. J. (1993) 'Depressive comorbidity in children and adolescents: empirical, theoretical and methodological issues.' *American Journal of Psychiatry 150,* 1779–1791.

Antonowicz, D. H. and Ross, R. R. (1994) 'Essential components of successful rehabilitation programs for offenders.' *International Journal of Offender Therapy and Comparative Criminology 38,* 2, 97–104.

APA (1994) *Diagnostic and Statistical Manual of Mental Disorders.* (Fourth edition) Arlington, VA: American Psychiatric Association.

Arbuthnot, J. and Gordon, D. A. (1986) 'Behavioral and cognitive effects of a moral reasoning development intervention for high-risk behavior disordered adolescents.' *Journal of Consulting and Clinical Psychology 54,* 2, 208–216.

Audit Commission (1996) *Misspent Youth. Young People and Crime.* London: Audit Commission.

Audit Commission (1999) *Children in Mind. Child and Adolescent Mental Health Services (CAMHS).* London: The Audit Commission for Local Authorities and the National Health Service in England and Wales.

Babinski, L. M., Hartsough, C. S. and Lambert, M. N. (1999) 'Childhood conduct problems, hyperactivity-impulsivity, and inattention as predictors of adult criminal activity.' *Journal of Child Psychology and Psychiatry 40,* 347–355.

Bagley, C. and Pritchard, C. (1998) 'The reduction of problem behaviours and school exclusion in at-risk youth: an experimental study of school social work with cost-benefit analyses.' *Child and Family Social Work 3,* 219–226.

Bailey, S. (1997) 'Sadistic and violent acts in the young.' *Child Psychology and Psychiatry Review 2,* 3, 92–102.

Bailey, V. F. A. (1996) 'Intensive interventions in conduct disorders.' *Archives of Disease in Childhood 74*, 4, 352–356.

Bank, L., Marlowe, H. J., Reid, J. B., Patterson, G. R. and Weinrott, M. R. (1991) 'A comparative evaluation of parent-training interventions for families of chronic delinquents.' *Journal of Abnormal Child Psychology 19*, 1, 15–33.

Barber, A. J., Tischler, V. A. and Healy, E. (2006) 'Consumer satisfaction and child behaviour problems in child and adolescent mental health services.' *Journal of Child Health Care 10*, 1, 9–21.

Barlow, J. (1999) *Systematic Review of the Effectiveness of Parent-Training Programmes in Improving Behaviour Problems in Children Aged 3–10 Years*, second edition. Oxford: Health Services Research Unit.

Barnes, D., Wistow, R., Dean, R. and Foster, B. (2005) *National Child and Adolescent Mental Health Service Mapping Exercise 2005. A Summary of National Trends.* Durham: Durham University School of Applied Social Sciences.

Barreto, S. J., Boekamp, J. R., Armstrong, L. M. and Gillen, P. (2004) 'Community-based interventions for juvenile firestarters: a brief family-centered model.' *Psychological Services 1*, 2, 158–168.

Barton, C., Alexander, J. F., Waldron, H., Turner, C. W. and Warburton, J. (1985) 'Generalizing treatment effects of Functional Family Therapy: three replications.' *American Journal of Family Therapy 13*, 16–26.

Baruch, G., Gerber, A. and Fearon, P. (1998) 'Adolescents who drop out of psychotherapy at a community-based psychotherapy centre: a preliminary investigation of the characteristics of early drop-outs, late drop-outs and those who continue treatment.' *British Journal of Medical Psychology 71*, 233–245.

Bassarath, L. (2003) 'Medication strategies in childhood aggression: a review.' *Canadian Journal of Psychiatry – Revue Canadienne de Psychiatrie 48*, 6, 367–373.

Battistich, V., Schaps, E., Watson, M. and Solomon, D. (1996) 'Prevention effects of the child development project: early findings from an ongoing multisite demonstration trial.' *Journal of Adolescent Research 11*, 1, 12–35.

Beck, R. and Fernandez, E. (1998) 'Cognitive-behavioral therapy in the treatment of anger: a meta-analysis.' *Cognitive Therapy and Research 22*, 1, 63–74.

Bedard, R. M., Rachel, M., Rosen, L. A. and Vacha-Haase, T. (2003) 'Wilderness therapy programs for juvenile delinquents: a meta-analysis.' *Journal of Therapeutic Wilderness Camping 3*, 1, 7–13.

Belfield, C. R., Nores, M., Barnett, S. and Schweinhart, L. J. (2006) 'The High/Scope Perry Preschool Program. Cost-benefit analysis using data from the age-40 followup.' *Journal of Human Resources 41*, 1, 162–190.

Bell, R. Q. (1968) 'A reinterpretation of the direction of effects in studies of socialization.' *Psychological Review 75*, 81–95.

Block, J. (1978) 'Effects of a rational emotive mental health program on poorly achieving, disruptive high school students.' *Journal of Counseling Psychology 25*, 61–65.

BMA Board of Science (2006) *Child and Adolescent Mental Health. A Guide for Healthcare Professionals.* London: British Medical Association.

Brennan, P. A., Grekin, E. R. and Mednick, S. A. (2003) 'Prenatal and perinatal influences on conduct disorder and serious delinquency.' In B. B. Lahey, T. E. Moffitt and A. Caspi (eds) *Causes of Conduct Disorder and Juvenile Delinquency*. New York: The Guilford Press, pp.319–341.

Brewer, D. D., Hawkins, J. D., Catalano, R. F. and Neckerman, H. J. (1995) 'Preventing serious, violent, and chronic juvenile offending. A review of evaluations of selected strategies in childhood, adolescence, and the community.' In J. C. Howell, B. Krisberg, J. D. Hawkins and J. J. Wilson (eds) *A Sourcebook: Serious, Violent and Chronic Juvenile Offenders*. London: Sage.

Brooks, R. (1994) 'Children at risk: fostering resilience and hope.' *American Journal of Orthopsychiatry 64*, 545–553.

Broota, A. and Sehgal, R. (2004) 'Management of conduct disorders through cognitive behavioural intervention [references].' *Psychological Studies 49*, 1, Jan-72.

Brown, S. A., Gleghorn, A., Schuckit, M., Myers, M. G. and Mott, M. A. (1996) 'Conduct disorder among adolescent substance abusers.' *Journal of the Study of Alcohol 57*, 314–324.

Bundy, C. (2004) 'Changing behaviour: using motivational interviewing techniques.' *Journal of the Royal Society of Medicine 97*, 43–47.

Burke, B. L., Arkowitz, H. and Menchola, M. (2003) 'The efficacy of motivational interviewing: a meta-analysis of controlled trials.' *Journal of Consulting and Clinical Psychology 71*, 5, 843–861.

Burke, J. D., Loeber, R. and Birmaher, B. (2003) 'Oppositional defiant disorder and conduct disorder: a review of the past 10 years, part II.' *Journal of the American Academy of Child and Adolescent Psychiatry 41*, 11, 1275–1293.

Camodeca, M. and Goossens, F. A. (2005) 'Aggression, social cognitions, anger and sadness in bullies and victims.' *Journal of Child Psychology and Psychiatry 46*, 2, 186–197.

Campbell, M., Cueva, J. E. and Adams, P. (1999) 'Pharmacotherapy of impulsive-aggressive behavior.' In C. R. Cloninger (ed) *Personality and Psychopathology.* New York: American Psychiatric Publishing Inc.

Campbell, M., Gonzalez, N. M. and Silva, N. N. (1992) 'The pharmacologic treatment of conduct disorders and rage outbursts.' *Pediatric Psychopharmacology 15*, 69–85.

Capaldi, D. M. and Patterson, G. R. (1987) 'An approach to the problem of recruitment and retention rates for longitudinal research strategies.' *Behavioral Assessment 9*, 169–177.

Caron, C. and Rutter, M. (1991) 'Comorbidity and child psychopathology: concepts, issues and research strategies.' *Journal of Child Psychology and Psychiatry and Allied Disciplines 32*, 1063–1080.

Chamberlain, P. (1990) 'Comparative evaluation of specialised foster care for seriously delinquent youths: a first step.' *Community Alternatives International Journal of Family Care 2*, 21–36.

Chamberlain, P. (1996) 'Intensified foster care: multi-level treatment for adolescents with conduct disorders in out-of-home care.' In E. D. Hibbs and P. S. Jensen (eds) *Psychosocial Treatments for Child and Adolescent Disorders.* Washington, DC: American Psychological Association, pp. 475–495.

Chamberlain, P. and Reid, J. B. (1991) 'Using a specialized foster care community treatment model for children and adolescents leaving the state mental hospital.' *Journal of Community Psychology 19*, 266–276.

Chamberlain, P. and Reid, J. B. (1998) 'Comparison of two community alternatives to incarceration for chronic juvenile offenders.' *Journal of Consulting and Clinical Psychology 66*, 4, 624–633.

Chamberlain, P. and Rosicky, J. G. (1995) 'The effectiveness of family therapy in the treatment of adolescents with conduct disorders and delinquency.' *Journal of Marital and Family Therapy 21*, 4, 441–459.

Cheng-Shannon, J., McGough, J. J., Pataki, C. and McCracken, J. T. (2004) 'Second-generation antipsychotic medications in children and adolescents [review] [200 refs].' *Journal of Child and Adolescent Psychopharmacology 14*, 3, 372–394.

Chiles, J. A., Miller, M. L. and Cox, G. B. (1980) 'Depression in an adolescent delinquent population.' *Archives of General Psychiatry 37*, 1179–1186.

Coffey, O. D. and Gemignani, M. G. (1994) *Effective Practices in Juvenile Correctional Education: A Study of the Literature and Research 1980–1992.* Washington, DC: Department of Justice.

Coleman, M., Pfeiffer, S. and Oakland, T. (1992) 'Aggression replacement training with behaviorally disordered adolescents.' *Behavioral Disorders 18*, 1, 54–66.

Connor, D. F., Barkley, R. A. and Davis, H. T. (2000) 'A pilot study of methylphenidate, clonidine, or the combination in ADHD comorbid with aggressive oppositional defiant or conduct disorder.' *Clinical Pediatrics* (Phila.), 15–25.

Cox, S. M., Davidson, W. S. and Bynum, T. S. (1995) 'A meta-analytic assessment of delinquency-related outcomes of alternative education programs.' *Crime and Delinquency 41*, 2, 219–234.

Curtis, N. M., Ronan, K. R. and Borduin, C. M. (2004) 'Multisystemic treatment: a meta-analysis of outcome studies.' *Journal of Family Psychology 18*, 3, 411–419.

Deeks, J. J., Altman, D. G. and Bradburn, M. J. (2001) 'Statistical methods for examining heterogeneity and combining results from several studies in meta-analysis.' In M. Egger, G. D. Smith and D. G. Altman (eds) *Systematic Reviews in Health Care. Meta-analysis in Context.* London: BMJ Publishing Group, pp.285–312.

Department for Education and Skills (2006a) *Care Matters: Transforming the Lives of Children and Young People in Care*. Norwich: The Stationery Office.

Department for Education and Skills (2006b) *Common Assessment Framework for Children and Young People: Practitioners' Guide*. London: DfES.

Department for Education and Skills (2006c) *Fact Sheet: Integrated Children's System*. London: DfES.

Department of Health (2004) *National Service Framework for Children, Young People and Maternity Services. The Mental Health and Psychological Well-being of Children and Young People*. London: Department of Health.

Dick, D. M., Viken, R. J., Kaprio, J., Pulkkinen, L. and Rose, R. J. (2005) 'Understanding the covariation among childhood externalizing symptoms: genetic and environmental influences on conduct disorder, attention deficit hyperactivity disorder, and oppositional defiant disorder symptoms.' *Journal of Abnormal Child Psychology 33*, 2, 219–229.

Disney, E. R., Elkins, I. J., McGue, M. and Iacono, W. G. (1999) 'Conduct disorder, and gender on substance use and abuse in adolescence.' *American Journal of Psychiatry 156*, 1515–1521.

Dodge, K. A. (2003) 'Do social information-processing patterns mediate aggressive behavior?' In B. B. Lahey, T. E. Moffitt and A. Caspi (eds) *Causes of Conduct Disorder and Juvenile Delinquency*. New York: The Guilford Press.

Dowden, C. and Andrews, D. A. (2003) 'Does family intervention work for delinquents? Results of a meta-analysis.' *Canadian Journal of Criminology and Criminal Justice 45*, 3, 327–342.

Dowden, C. and Andrews, D. A. (2004) 'The importance of staff practice in delivering effective correctional treatment: a meta-analytic review of core correctional practice.' *International Journal of Offender Therapy and Comparative Criminology 48*, 2, 203–214.

Dretzke, J., Frew, E., Davenport, C., Barlow, J., Stewart-Brown, S., Sandercock, J., Bayliss, S., Raftery, J., Hyde, C. and Taylor, R. (2005) *The Effectiveness and Cost-effectiveness of Parent Training/Education Programmes for the Treatment of Conduct Disorder, Including Oppositional Defiant Disorder, in Children*. York: Health Technology Assessment NHS R&D HTA Programme.

Drotar, D., Stein, R. E. K. and Perrin, E. C. (1995) 'Methodological issues in using the Child Behavior Checklist and its related instruments in clinical child psychology research.' *Journal of Clinical Child Psychology 24*, 2, 184–194.

Dumas, J. E. and Wahler, R. G. (1983) 'Predictors of treatment outcome in parent training: mother insularity and socioeconomic disadvantage.' *Behavioral Assessment 5*, 301–313.

Dush, C. M., Hirt, M. L. and Schroeder, H. E. (1989) 'Self-statement modification in the treatment of child-behavior disorders – a meta-analysis.' *Psychological Bulletin 106*, 97–106.

Eddy, J. M., Reid, J. B., Stoolmiller, M. and Fetrow, R. A. (2003) 'Outcomes during middle school for an elementary school-based preventive intervention for conduct problems: follow-up results from a randomised trial.' *Behavior Therapy 34*, 535–552.

Eddy, J. M., Whaley, B. and Chamberlain, P. (2004) 'The prevention of violent behavior by chronic and serious male juvenile offenders: a 2-year follow-up of a randomized clinical trial.' *Journal of Emotional and Behavioral Disorders 12*, 1, 2–8.

Ekeland, E., Jamtvedt, G., Heian, F. and Hagen, K. B. (2006) *Exercise for Oppositional Defiant Disorder and Conduct Disorder in Children and Adolescents (Protocol)*. Cochrane Database of Systematic Reviews.

Ercan, S. E., Kutlu, A., Cikoglu, S., Veznedaroglu, B., Erermis, S. and Varan, A. (2003) 'Risperidone in children and adolescents with conduct disorder: a single-center, open-label study.' *Current Therapeutic Research 64*, 1, 55–64.

Etscheid, S. (1991) 'Reducing aggressive behaviour and improving self-control: a cognitive-behavioural training program for behaviorally disordered adolescents.' *Behavioural Disorders 16*, 2, pp.107–155.

Faraone, S. V., Biederman, J., Keenan, K. and Tsuang, M. T. (1991) 'Separation of DSM-III attention deficit disorder and conduct disorder: evidence from a family genetic study of American child psychiatry patients.' *Psychological Medicine 21*, 109–121.

Farrington, D. (1989) 'Early predictors of adolescent aggression and adult violence.' *Violence and Victims 4*, 79–100.

Farrington, D. and Welsh, B. C. (2002) 'Family-based crime prevention.' In L. W. Sherman, D. Farrington, B. C. Welsh and D. Layton MacKenzie (eds) *Evidence-based Crime Prevention*. London: Routledge.

Farrington, D. P. (1995) 'The twelfth Jack Tizard memorial lecture. The development of offending and antisocial behaviour from childhood: key findings from the Cambridge study in delinquent development.' *Journal of Child Psychology and Psychiatry 360*, 6, 929–964.

Farrington, D. P., Loeber, R. and Van Kammen, W. B. (1990) 'Long-term criminal outcomes of hyperactivity-impulsivity-attention deficit and conduct problems in childhood.' In L. N. Robins and M. Rutter (eds) *Straight and Devious Pathways from Childhood to Adulthood.* Cambridge: Cambridge University Press, pp.63–81.

Feilzer, M., Appleton, C., Roberts, C. and Hoyle, C. (2004) *Cognitive Behaviour Projects. The National Evaluation of the Youth Justice Board's Cognitive Behaviour Projects.* London: Youth Justice Board.

Feldman, M. and Wilson, A. (1997) 'Adolescent suicidality in urban minorities and its relationship to conduct disorders, depression, and separation anxiety.' *Journal of the American Academy of Child and Adolescent Psychiatry 36*, 75–84.

Findling, R. L., Kusumakar, V., Daneman, D., Moshang, T., De Smedt, G. and Binder, C. (2003) 'Prolactin levels during long-term risperidone treatment in children and adolescents.' *Journal of Clinical Psychiatry 64*, 11, 1362–1369.

Fonagy, P., Target, M., Cottrell, D., Phillips, J. and Kurtz, Z. (2002) *What Works for Whom? A Critical Review of Treatments for Children and Adolescents.* New York: Guilford Press.

Ford, T. and Nikapota, A. (2000) 'Teachers' attitudes towards child mental health services.' *Psychiatric Bulletin 24*, 457–461.

Foreman, D. M. (2001) 'General practitioners and child and adolescent psychiatry: awareness and training of the new commissioners.' *Psychiatric Bulletin 25*, 101–104.

Fox, C. and Hawton, K. (2004) *Deliberate Self-harm in Adolescence.* London: Jessica Kingsley Publishers.

Franklin, G. A., Pucci, P. S., Arbabi, S., Brandt, M.-M., Wahl, W. L. and Taheri, P. A. (2002) 'Decreased juvenile arson and firesetting recidivism after implementation of a multidisciplinary prevention program.' *Journal of TRAUMA Injury, Infection, and Critical Care 53*, 2, 260–266.

Frick, P. J. (2001) 'Effective interventions for children and adolescents with conduct disorder.' *Canadian Journal of Psychiatry – Revue Canadienne de Psychiatrie 46*, 7, 597–608.

Gass, M. A. (1993) 'Foundations of adventure therapy.' In M. A. Gass (ed) *Adventure Therapy: Therapeutic Applications of Adventure Programming.* Dubuque, IA: Kendall Hunt Publishing Company, pp.3–10.

Gérardin, P., Cohen, D., Mazet, P. and Flament, M. F. (2002) 'Drug treatment of conduct disorder in young people.' *European Neuropsychopharmacology 12*, 5, 361–370.

Gesch, B. C., Hammond, S. M., Hampson, S. E., Eves, A. and Crowder, M. J. (2002) 'Influence of supplementary vitamins, minerals and essential fatty acids on the antisocial behaviour of young adult prisoners.' *British Journal of Psychiatry 181*, 22–28.

Gilmour, J., Hill, B., Place, M. and Skuse, D. H. (2004) 'Social communication deficits in conduct disorder: a clinical and community survey.' *Journal of Child Psychology and Psychiatry 45*, 5, 967–978.

Goldstein, A. P. and Glick, B. (1994) *The Prosocial Gang. Implementing Aggression Replacement Training.* Thousand Oaks: Sage.

Goodman, R. (1997) 'The strengths/difficulties questionnaire.' *Journal of Child Psychology and Psychiatry 38*, 5, 581–586.

Gottfredson, D., Wilson, D. B. and Skroban Najaka, S. (2002) 'School-based crime prevention.' In L. W. Sherman, D. Farrington, B. C. Welsh and D. Layton MacKenzie (eds) *Evidence-based Crime Prevention.* London: Routledge, pp.56–164.

Green, H., McGinnity, A., Meltzer, H., Ford, T. and Goodman, R. (2005) *Mental Health of Children and Young People in Great Britain, 2004. Office for National Statistics on behalf of the Department of Health and the Scottish Executive.* London: Palgrave Macmillan.

Greene, R. W., Biederman, J., Zerwas, S., Monuteaux, M. C., Goring, J. C. and Faraone, S. V. (2002) 'Psychiatric comorbidity, family dysfunction, and social impairment in referred youth with oppositional defiant disorder.' *American Journal of Psychiatry 159*, 7, 1214–1224.

Gundersen, K. and Svartdal, F. (2006) 'Aggression replacement training in Norway: outcome evaluation of 11 Norwegian student projects.' *Scandinavian Journal of Educational Research 50*, 1, 63–81.

Hagell, A. (2002) *The Mental Health of Young Offenders. Bright Futures: Working with Vulnerable Young People*. London: The Mental Health Foundation, August.

Hahn, R. A., *et al.* and CDC Task Force on Community Preventive Services (2004) 'Therapeutic foster care for the prevention of violence: a report on recommendations of the Task Force on Community Preventive Services.' *Morbidity and Mortality Weekly Report 53*, RR–10, 1–8.

Harrington, R. (2000) 'Cognitive-behavioural therapies for children and adolescents.' In M. G. Gelder, J. J. Lopez-Ibor and N. C. Andreasen (eds) *New Oxford Textbook of Psychiatry*. New York: Oxford University Press.

Harrington, R. and Bailey, S. (2003) *The Scope for Preventing Antisocial Personality Disorder by Intervening in Adolescence*. Liverpool: National R&D Programme on Forensic Mental Health.

Hazell, P. L. and Stuart, J. E. (2003) 'A randomized controlled trial of clonidine added to psychostimulant medication for hyperactive and aggressive children.' *Journal of the American Academy of Child and Adolescent Psychiatry 42*, 8, 886–894.

Henggeler, S. W. and Borduin, C. M. (1990) *Family Therapy and Beyond: A Multisystemic Approach to Treating the Behavior Problems of Children and Adolescents*. Pacific Grove, CA: Brooks/Cole.

Henggeler, S. W., Schoenwald, S. K. and Borduin, C. M. (1998) *Multisystemic Treatment of Antisocial Behaviour in Children and Adolescents*. New York: The Guilford Press.

Hill-Tout, J., Pithouse, A. and Lowe, K. (2003) 'Training foster carers in a preventive approach to children who challenge: mixed messages from research.' *Adoption and Fostering 27*, 1, 47–56.

Home Office (1997) *No More Excuses – A New Approach to Tackling Youth Crime in England and Wales*. London: Home Office.

Hoover, D. (2003) 'A tangled web: responders struggle to stop juvenile firesetting.' *Every Second Counts 5*, 1.

House of Commons Health Committee (1997) *Child and Adolescent Mental Health Services. Health Committee Fourth Report: Session 1996–97*. London: House of Commons, HC26-I.

Ishikawa, S. S. and Raine, A. (2003) 'Prefrontal deficits and antisocial behavior. A causal model.' In B. B. Lahey, T. E. Moffitt and A. Caspi (eds) *Causes of Conduct Disorder and Juvenile Delinquency*. New York: The Guilford Press, pp.277–304.

Izzo, R. L. and Ross, R. R. (1990) 'Meta-analysis of rehabilitation programs for juvenile delinquents: a brief report.' *Criminal Justice and Behavior 17*, 1, 134–142.

Kaplan, B. J., Fisher, J. E., Crawford, S. G., Field, C. J. and Kolb, B. (2004) 'Improved mood and behavior during treatment with a mineral-vitamin supplement: an open-label case series of children.' *Journal of Child and Adolescent Psychopharmacology 14*, 1, 115–122.

Kavale, K. A., Mathur, S. R., Forness, S. R. and Rutherford, M. M. (1997) 'Effectiveness of social skills training for students with behavior disorders: a meta-analysis.' *Advances in Learning and Behavioral Disabilities 11*, 1–26.

Kazdin, A. E. (1995) *Conduct Disorder in Childhood and Adolescence*, second edition. Thousand Oaks, CA: Sage.

Kazdin, A. E. (2001) 'Treatment of conduct disorder.' In J. Hill and B. Maughan (eds) *Conduct Disorder in Childhood and Adolescence*. Cambridge: Cambridge University Press.

Kazdin, A. E., Holland, L. and Crowley, M. (1997) 'Family experience of barriers to treatment and premature termination from child therapy.' *Journal of Consulting and Clinical Psychology 65*, 3, 453–463.

Kazdin, A. E. and Weisz, J. R. (2003) *Evidence-based Psychotherapies for Children and Adolescents*. New York: Guilford Press.

Keegan Eamon, M. and Venkataraman, M. (2003) 'Implementing parent management training in the context of poverty.' *The American Journal of Family Therapy 31*, 281–293.

Kellermann, A. (1998) 'Preventing youth violence: what works.' *Annual Review of Public Health 19*, 271–292.

Kelly, C., Allan, S., Roscoe, P. and Herrick, E. (2003) 'The mental health needs of looked after children: an integrated multi-agency model of care.' *Clinical Child Psychology and Psychiatry 8*, 3, 323–335.

Kerfoot, M., Panayiotopoulos, C. and Harrington, R. (2004) 'Social services and CAMHS: a national survey.' *Child and Adolescent Mental Health 9*, 4, 162–167.

Kingston, L. and Prior, M. (1995) 'The development of patterns of stable, transient, and school age aggressive behaviour in young children.' *Journal of Archives of Academic Child and Adolescent Psychiatry 34*, 348–358.

Kolko, D. J. (2001) 'Efficacy of cognitive-behavioral treatment and fire safety education for children who set fires: initial and follow-up outcomes.' *Journal of Child Psychology and Psychiatry 42*, 3, 359–369.

Kurtz, A. (2002) 'What works for delinquency? The effectiveness of interventions for teenage offending behaviour.' *Journal of Forensic Psychiatry 13*, 3, 671–692.

Lahey, B. B., Loeber, R. and Frick, P. J. (1992) 'Oppositional defiant and conduct disorders: issues to be resolved for DSM-IV.' *Journal of American Academy of Child and Adolescent Psychiatry 31*, 539–546.

Lahey, B. B., Loeber, R., Hart, E. L., Frick, P. J. and Applegate, B. (1995) 'Four-year longitudinal study of conduct disorder in boys: patterns and predictors of persistence.' *Journal of Abnormal Child Psychology 104*, 83–93.

Lahey, B. B., Moffitt, T. E. and Caspi, A. (2003) *Causes of Conduct Disorder and Juvenile Delinquency*. New York: The Guilford Press.

Lahey, B. B. and Waldman, I. D. (2003) 'A developmental propensity model of the origins of conduct problems during childhood and adolescence.' In B. B. Lahey, T. E. Moffitt and A. Caspi (eds) *Causes of Conduct Disorder and Juvenile Delinquency*. New York: The Guilford Press, pp.76–117.

Latimer, J. (2001) 'A meta-analytic examination of youth delinquency, family treatment, and recidivism.' *Canadian Journal of Criminology 43*, 2, 237–253.

Lavin, M. and Rifkin, A. (1993) 'Diagnosis and pharmacotherapy of conduct disorder.' *Programme of Neuropsychopharmacological Biology Psychiatry 17*, 875–885.

Layton MacKenzie, D. (2002) 'Reducing criminal activities of known offenders and delinquents: crime prevention in the courts and corrections.' In L. W. Sherman, D. Farrington, B. C. Welsh and D. Layton MacKenzie (eds) *Evidence-based Crime Prevention*. London: Routledge, pp.330–404.

Lee, C. L. and Bates, J. E. (1985) 'Mother–child interaction at two years and perceived difficult temperament.' *Child Development 50*, 134–325.

Lees, J., Manning, N. and Rawlings, B. (1999) *Therapeutic Community Effectiveness: A Systematic International Review of Therapeutic Community Treatment for People with Personality Disorders and Mentally Disordered Offenders*. York: NHS Centre for Reviews and Dissemination (CRD), 17.

Lees, J., Manning, N. and Rawlings, B. A. (2004) 'A culture of enquiry: research evidence and the therapeutic community.' *Psychiatric Quarterly 75*, 3, 279–294.

Liabo, K., Gibbs, J. and Underdown, A. (2004) *Group-based Parenting Programmes and Reducing Children's Behaviour Problems*. London: National Children's Bureau, 211.

Liddle, M. (1999) *Wasted Lives. Counting the Cost of Juvenile Offending*. London: National Association for the Care and Resettlement of Offenders.

Lipsey, M. W. (1992) 'Juvenile delinquency treatment: a meta-analytic inquiry into the variability of effects.' In T. A. Cook and O. And (eds) *Meta-analysis for Explanation: A Casebook*. New York: Russel Sage Foundation, pp.83–127.

Lipsey, M. W. (1995) 'What do we learn from 400 research studies on the effectiveness of treatment with juvenile delinquents?' In J. McGuire (ed) *What Works: Reducing Reoffending: Guidelines from Research and Practice*. Oxford: John Wiley and Sons Ltd.

Lipsey, M. W., Chapman, G. L. and Landenberger, N. A. (2001) 'Cognitive-behavioral programs for offenders.' *Annals of the American Academy of Political and Social Science 578*, November, 144–157.

Lipsey, M. W. and Wilson, D. B. (1998) 'Effective intervention for serious juvenile offenders: a synthesis of research.' In R. Loeber and D. Farrington (eds) *Serious and Violent Juvenile Offenders: Risk Factors and Successful Interventions*. Thousand Oaks, CA: Sage Publications.

Littell, J. H. (2005) 'Multisystemic treatment for social, emotional, and behavioral problems in children and adolescents aged 10–17 (review).' *Cochrane Database of Systematic Reviews 1*, 4, 1–42.

Liu, J., Raine, A., Venables, P. H. and Mednick, S. A. (2004) 'Malnutrition at age 3 years and externalizing behavior problems at ages 8, 11, and 17 years.' *American Journal of Psychiatry 161*, 2005–2013.

Lochman, J. E. and Salekin, R. T. (2003) 'Introduction: prevention and intervention with aggressive and disruptive children: next steps in behavioral intervention research.' *Behavior Therapy 34*, 4, 413–420.

Loeber, R. (1982) 'The stability of antisocial and delinquent child behaviour: a review.' *Child Development 53*, 1431–1446.

Loeber, R. and Stouthamer-Loeber, M. (1986) 'Family factors as correlates and predictors of juvenile conduct problems and delinquency.' In M. Tonry and N. Morris (eds) *Crime and Justice*, vol. 7. Chicago: University of Chicago Press, pp.29–149.

Lösel, F. and Beelmann, A. (2003) 'Effects of child skills training in preventing antisocial behavior: a systematic review of randomized evaluations.' *Annals of the American Academy of Political and Social Science 587*, May, 84–109.

Lowe, L. A. (1998) 'Using the Child Behavior checklist in assessing conduct disorder: issues of reliability and validity.' *Research on Social Work Practice 8*, 3, 286–301.

Mabe, P. A., Turner, K. M. and Josephson, A. M. (2001) 'Parent management training.' *Current Perspectives on Family Therapy 10*, 3, 451–464.

MacDonald, V. M. and Achenbach, T. M. (1999) 'Attention problems as 6-year predictors of signs of disturbance in a national sample.' *Journal of American Academy of Child and Adolescent Psychiatry 38*, 1254–1261.

Marriage, K., Fine, S. and Moretti, M. (1986) 'Relationship between depression and conduct disorder in children and adolescents.' *Journal of the American Academy of Child Psychiatry 25*, 687–691.

Marshall, J. and Watt, P. (1999) *Child Behaviour Problems: A Literature Review of the Size and Nature of the Problem and Prevention Interventions in Childhood.* Perth, Australia: The Interagency Committee on Children's Futures.

Masten, A. S., Burt, K. B., Roisman, G. I., Obradoviæ, J., Long, J. D. and Tellegen, A. (2004) 'Resource and resilience in the transition to adulthood: continuity and change.' *Development and Psychopathology 16*, 1071–1094.

Maughan, B., Rowe, R., Messer, J., Goodman, R. and Meltzer, H. (2004) 'Conduct disorder and oppositional defiant disorder in a national sample: developmental epidemiology.' *Journal of Child Psychology and Psychiatry 45*, 3, 609–621.

Maughan, B. and Rutter, M. (1998) 'Continuities and discontinuities in antisocial behaviour from childhood to adult life.' *Clinical Child Psychology 20*, 1–47.

McArdle, P., O'Brien, G. and Kolvin, I. (1995) 'Hyperactivity: prevalence and relationship with conduct disorder.' *Journal of Child and Adolescent Psychiatry 36*, 279–303.

McCord, J., Spatz Widom, C. and Crowell, N. A. (2001) *Juvenile Crime. Juvenile Justice.* Washington DC: National Academy Press.

McLaren, K. (1992) *Reducing Reoffending: What Works Now.* Wellington, NZ: Penal Division, New Zealand Department of Justice.

McMahon, R. J. and Forehand, R. (1984) 'Parent training for the noncompliant child: treatment outcome, generalization, and adjunct therapy procedures.' In R. F. Dangel and R. A. Polster (eds) *Parent Training.* New York: The Guilford Press.

Meltzer, H., Gatward, R., Corbin, T., Goodman, R. and Ford, T. (2002) *The Mental Health of Young People Looked After by Local Authorities in England.* London: Office for National Statistics.

Meltzer, H., Lader, D., Corbin, T., Goodman, R. and Ford, T. (2004a) *The Mental Health of Young People Looked After by Local Authorities in Scotland.* London: Office for National Statistics.

Meltzer, H., Lader, D., Corbin, T., Goodman, R. and Ford, T. (2004b) *The Mental Health of Young People Looked After by Local Authorities in Wales.* London: Office for National Statistics.

Meyer, J. M., Rutter, M., Silberg, J. L., Maes, H. H., Simonoff, E., Shillady, L. L., Pickles, A., Hewitt, J. K. and Eaves, L. J. (2000) 'Familial aggregation for conduct disorder symptomology: the role of genes, marital discord and family adaptability.' *Psychological Medicine 30*, 759–774.

Miller, W. R. and Rollnick, S. (2002) *Motivational Interviewing: Preparing People to Change Addictive Behaviour.* New York: The Guilford Press.

Miller-Johnson, S., Coie, J. D., Maumary-Gremaud, A., Bierman, K. and The Conduct Problems Prevention Research Group (2002) 'Peer rejection and aggression and early starter models of conduct disorder.' *Journal of Abnormal Child Psychology 30*, 3, 217–230.

Moffitt, T. E. (2003) 'Life-course persistent and adolescence-limited antisocial behavior.' In B. B. Lahey, T. E. Moffitt and A. Caspi (eds) *Causes of Conduct Disorder and Juvenile Delinquency.* New York: The Guilford Press, pp.49–75.

Moffitt, T. E., Caspi, A., Dickson, N., Silva P. and Stanton, W. (1996) 'Childhood-onset versus adolescent antisocial conduct problems in males: natural history from ages 3 to 18 years.' *Development and Psychopathology 8*, 2, 399–424.

Montgomery, P. (2005) *Media-based Behavioural Treatments for Behavioural Disorders in Children.* Oxford: The Cochrane Library.

Moretti, M. M., Emmrys, C., Grizenko, N., Holland, R., Moore, K., Shamsie, J. and Hamilton, H. (1997) 'The treatment of conduct disorder: perspectives from across Canada.' *Canadian Journal of Psychiatry 42*, 637–648.

Morrell, J. and Murray, L. (2003) 'Parenting and the development of conduct disorder and hyperactive symptoms in childhood: a prospective longitudinal study from 2 months to 8 years.' *Journal of Child Psychology and Psychiatry 44*, 4, 489–508.

Myers, M. G., Stewart, D. G. and Brown, S. A. (1998) 'Progression from conduct disorder to antisocial personality disorder following treatment for adolescent substance abuse.' *American Journal of Psychiatry 155*, 4, 479–485.

Mytton, J. A., DiGuiseppi, C., Gough, D. A., Taylor, R. S. and Logan, S. (2006) 'School-based secondary prevention programmes for preventing violence.' *Cochrane Database of Systematic Reviews 3.*

NACRO (2004) *Youth Crime Briefing. Some Facts About Children and Young People Who Offend – 2004.* London: Nacro Youth Crime.

National Institute for Health and Clinical Excellence (2006) *Parent-Training/Education Programmes in the Management of Children with Conduct Disorder.* London: NICE technology appraisal guidance 102.

National Statistics (2000) *Mental Disorder Among Young Offenders.* London: National Statistics.

Nickel, M., Luley, J., Krawczyk, J., Nickel, C., Widermann, C., Lahmann, C., Muehlbacher, M., Forthuber, P., Kettler, C., Leiberich, P., Tritt, K., Mitterlehner, F., Kaplan, P., Pedrosa Gil, F., Rother, W. and Loew, T. (2006) 'Bullying girls – changes after brief strategic family therapy: a randomized, prospective, controlled trial with one-year follow-up.' *Psychotherapy and Psychosomatics 75*, 47–55.

Nickel, M. K., Krawczyk, J., Nickel, C., Forthuber, P., Kettler, C., Leiberich, P., Muehlbacher, M., Tritt, K., Mitterlehner, F. O., Lahmann, C., Rother, W. K. and Loew, T. H. (2004) 'Anger, interpersonal relationships, and health-related quality of life in bullying boys who are treated with outpatient family therapy: a randomized, prospective, controlled trial with 1 year of follow-up.' *Pediatrics 116*, 247–254.

Nigg, J. T. and Huang-Pollock, C. L. (2003) 'An early-onset model of the role of executive functions and intelligence in conduct disorder/delinquency.' In B. B. Lahey, T. E. Moffitt and A. Caspi (eds) *Causes of Conduct Disorder and Juvenile Delinquency.* New York: The Guilford Press, pp.227–253.

Nugent, W. R., Bruley, C. and Allen, P. (1998) 'The effects of aggression replacement training on antisocial behavior in a runaway shelter.' *Research on Social Work Practice 8*, 6, 637–656.

Oakley, A., Hickey, D. and Rajan, L. (1996) 'Social support in pregnancy: does it have long-term effects?' *Journal of Reproductive and Infant Psychology 14*, 7–22.

Oakley, A., Rajan, L. and Grant, A. (1990) 'Social support and pregnancy outcome.' *British Journal of Obstetrics and Gynaecology 97*, 155–162.

Ogden, T. and Halliday-Boykins, C. (2004) 'Multisystemic treatment of antisocial adolescents in Norway: replication of clinical outcomes outside of the US.' *Child and Adolescent Mental Health 9*, 2, 77–83.

Olds, D., Henderson, C. R., Charles, R., Cole, R., Eckenrode, J., Kitzman, H., Luckey, D., Pettitt, L., Sidora, K., Morris, P. and Powers, J. (1998) 'Long-term effects of nurse home visitation on children's criminal and antisocial behavior: 15-year follow-up from a randomized controlled trial.' *Journal of the American Medical Association 280*, 14, 1238–1244.

Olweus, D. (1991) 'Bully/victim problems among school children: basic facts and effects of a school-based intervention program.' In D. J. Pepler and K. H. Rubin (eds) *The Development and Treatment of Childhood Aggression.* Hillsdale, NJ: Lawrence Erlbaum Associates.

Olweus, D. (1994) 'Annotation: bullying at school: basic facts and effects of a school based intervention program.' *Journal of Child Psychology and Psychiatry 35*, 7, 1171–1190.

Ortega, R. and Lera, M.-J. (2000) 'The Seville anti-bullying in school project.' *Aggressive Behavior 26*, 113–123.

Palmer, E. J., Caulfield, L. S. and Hollin, C. R. (2005) *Evaluations of Interventions with Arsonists and Young Firesetters.* London: Office of the Deputy Prime Minister.

Patterson, G. R. (1982) *A Social Learning Approach to Family Intervention: III. Coercive Family Process.* Eugene, OR: Castalia.

Patterson, G. R., DeBaryshe, D. and Ramsey, E. (1989) 'A developmental perspective on antisocial behaviour.' *American Psychologist 44,* 2, 329–335.

Patterson, G. R., Dishion, T. J. and Chamberlain, P. (1993) 'Outcomes and methodological issues relating to treatment of antisocial children.' In T. R. Giles (ed) *Handbook of Effective Psychotherapy.* New York: Plenum Press.

Percy-Smith, J. (2005) *What Works in Strategic Partnerships for Children?* Barkingside: Barnardo's.

Peters, S., Calam, R. and Harrington, R. (2005) 'Maternal attributions and expressed emotion as predictors of attendance at parent management training.' *Journal of Child Psychology and Psychiatry 46,* 4, 436–448.

Petras, H., Schaeffer, C. M., Ialongo, N., Hubbard, S., Muthen, B., Lambert, S. F., Poduska, J. and Kellam, S. (2004) 'When the course of aggressive behavior in childhood does not predict antisocial outcomes in adolescence and young adulthood: an examination of potential explanatory variables.' *Development and Psychopathology 16,* 919–941.

Petrosino, A. (1997) *What Works Revisited Again: A Meta-analysis of Randomized Experiments in Delinquency Prevention, Rehabilitation and Deterrence.* New Jersey: Rutgers University.

Petrosino, A., Turpin-Petrosino, C. and Buehler, J. (2004) '"Scared Straight" and other juvenile awareness programs for preventing juvenile delinquency.' *Cochrane Database of Systematic Reviews.*

Petticrew, M. and Roberts, H. (2003) 'Evidence, hierarchies and typologies: horses for courses.' *Journal of Epidemiology and Community Health 57,* 527–529.

Petticrew, M. and Roberts, H. (2006) *Systematic Reviews in the Social Sciences. A Practical Guide.* Oxford: Blackwell Publishing.

Platt, J. E., Campbell, M., Grega, D. M. and Green, W. H. (1984) 'Cognitive effects of haloperidol and lithium in aggressive conduct-disorder children.' *Psychopharmacological Bulletin 20,* 93–97.

Pote, H., Stratton, P., Cottrell, D., Shapiro, C. D. and Boston, P. (2003) 'Systemic family therapy can be manualized: research process and findings.' *Journal of Family Therapy 25,* 236–262.

Potter, R., Langley, K. and Sakhuja, D. (2005) 'All things to all people: what referrers want from their child and adolescent mental health service.' *Psychiatric Bulletin 29,* 262–265.

Poyner, B. (1993) 'What works in crime prevention: an overview of evaluations.' In R. V. Clarke (ed.) *Crime Prevention Studies: Vol. 1.* Monsey, NY: Criminal Justice Press, pp.7–34.

Pritchard, C. (2001) *A Family–Teacher–Social Work Alliance to Reduce Truancy and Delinquency – the Dorset Healthy Alliance Project.* London: Home Office Research Development and Statistics Directorate.

Raue, J. and Spence, S. H. (1985) 'Group versus individual applications of reciprocity training for parent-youth conflict.' *Behavior Research and Therapy 23,* 177–186.

Reddy, L. A. and Pfeiffer, S. I. (1997) 'Effectiveness of treatment foster care with children and adolescents: a review of outcome studies.' *Journal of the American Academy of Child and Adolescent Psychiatry 36,* 581–588.

Redondo, S., Sanchez-Meca, J. and Garrido, V. (1999) 'The influence of treatment programmes on the recidivism of juvenile and adult offenders: a European meta-analytic review.' *Psychology, Crime and Law 5,* 3, 251–278.

Reid, M. J., Webster-Stratton, C. and Baydar, N. (2004) 'Halting the development of conduct problems in head start children: the effects of parent training.' *Journal of Clinical Child and Adolescent Psychology 33,* 2, 279–291.

Reinecke, M. A. (1995) 'Comorbidity of conduct disorder and depression among adolescents: implications for assessment and treatment.' *Cognitive and Behavioral Practice 2,* 299–326.

Renaud, J., Brent, D., Birmaher, B., Chiappetta, L. and Bridge, J. (1999) 'Suicide in adolescents with disruptive disorder.' *Journal of the American Academy of Child and Adolescent Psychiatry 38,* 846–851.

Rey, J. M. (1994) 'Comorbidity between disruptive disorders and depression in referred adolescents.' *Australian and New Zealand Journal of Psychiatry 28,* 106–113.

Reyes, M., Buitelaar, J., Toren, P., Augustyns, I. and Eerdekens, M. (2006) 'A randomized, double-blind, placebo-controlled study of risperidone maintenance treatment in children and adolescents with disruptive behavior disorders.' *American Journal of Psychiatry 163*, 3, 402–410.

Rhee, S. H. and Waldman, I. D. (2003) 'Testing alternative hypotheses regarding the role of development on genetic and environmental influences underlying antisocial behavior.' In B. B. Lahey, T. E. Moffitt and A. Caspi (eds) *Causes of Conduct Disorder and Juvenile Delinquency.* New York: The Guilford Press, pp.305–318.

Rhode, P., Clarke, G. N., Mace, D. E., Jorgensen, J. S. and Seeley, J. R. (2004) 'An efficacy/effectiveness study of cognitive-behavioral treatment for adolescents with comorbid major depression and conduct disorder.' *Journal of the American Academy of Child and Adolescent Psychiatry 43*, 6, 660–668.

Richardson, G. J. R. and Partridge, I. (2000) 'Child and adolescent mental health services liaison with Tier 1 services. A consultation exercise with school nurses.' *Psychiatric Bulletin 24*, 462–463.

Richardson, J. and Joughin, C. (2002) *Parent-training Programmes for the Management of Young Children with Conduct Disorders. Findings from Research.* London: Gaskell, The Royal College of Psychiatrists.

Richman, N., Stevenson, J. and Graham, P. J. (1982) *Pre-school to School: A Behavioural Study.* London: Academic Press.

Richters, J. E. and Cicchetti, D. (1993) 'Mark Twain meets DSM-III-R: conduct disorder, development, and the concept of harmful dysfunction.' *Development and Psychopathology 5*, 5–29.

Rigby, K. (2002) *A Meta-evaluation of Methods and Approaches to Reducing Bullying in Pre-schools and Early Primary School in Australia.* Canberra: Attorney-General's Department.

Riggs, P. D., Mikulich, S. K. and Hall, S. K. (2001) 'Effects of pemoline on ADHD, antisocial behaviors and substance use in adolescents with conduct disorder and substance use disorder.' *Drug and Alcohol Dependence 63*, Suppl 1, 16–21.

Roberts, A. R. and Camasso, M. J. (1991) 'The effect of juvenile offender treatment programs on recidivism: a meta-analysis of 46 studies.' *Notre Dame Journal of Law, Ethics and Public Policy 5*, 2, 421–441.

Roberts, H., Liabo, K., Lucas, P., DuBois, D. and Sheldon, T. A. (2004) 'Mentoring to reduce antisocial behaviour in childhood.' *British Medical Journal 328*, 512–514.

Robins, L. N. (1966) *Deviant Children Grown Up: A Sociological and Psychiatric Study of Sociopathic Personality.* Baltimore, MD: Williams and Wilkins.

Robins, L. N. (1978) 'Sturdy childhood predictors of adult antisocial behaviour: replications from longitudinal studies.' *Psychological Medicine 8*, 611–622.

Robins, L. N. (1991) 'Conduct disorder.' *Journal of Child Psychology and Psychiatry 32*, 193–212.

Robins, L. N. and McEvoy, L. (1990) 'Conduct problems as predictors of substance abuse.' In L. N. Robins and M. Rutter (eds) *Straight and Devious Pathways from Childhood to Adulthood.* Cambridge: Cambridge University Press.

Roland, E. (1993) 'Bullying: a developing tradition of research and management.' In D. P. Tattum (ed.) *Understanding and Managing Bullying.* Oxford: Heinemann Educational.

Rutter, M. (1996) 'Connections between child and adult psychopathy.' *European Child and Adolescent Psychiatry 5*, 1, 4–7.

Rutter, M. (1999) 'Psychosocial adversity and child psychopathology.' *British Journal of Psychiatry 174*, 6, 480–493.

Rutter, M. (2003a) 'Commentary: causal processes leading to antisocial behavior.' *Developmental Psychology 39*, 2, 372–378.

Rutter, M. (2003b) 'Crucial paths from risk indicator to causal mechanism.' In B. B. Lahey, T. E. Moffitt and A. Caspi (eds) *Causes of Conduct Disorder and Juvenile Delinquency.* New York: The Guilford Press, pp.3–24.

Rutter, M. (2005) 'How the environment affects mental health.' *British Journal of Psychiatry 186*, 4–6.

Rutter, M. and Giller, H. (1983) *Juvenile Delinquency Trends and Perspectives.* New York: Penguin Books.

Rutter, M., Giller, H. and Hagell, A. (1998) *Antisocial Behaviour by Young People.* Cambridge: Cambridge University Press.

Salmon, G. and Rapport, F. (2005) 'Multi-agency voices: a thematic analysis of multi-agency working practices within the setting of a child and adolescent mental health service.' *Journal of Interprofessional Care 19,* 5, 429–443.

Sameroff, A. J., Peck, S. C. and Eccles, J. S. (2004) 'Changing ecological determinants of conduct problems from early adolescence to early adulthood.' *Development and Psychopathology 16,* 873–896.

Sanson, A., Smart, D., Prior, M. and Oberklaid, F. (1993) 'Precursors of hyperactivity and aggression.' *Journal of the American Academy of Child and Adolescent Psychiatry 32,* 1207–1216.

Santisteban, D. A., Coatsworth, J. D., Perez-Vidal, A., Mitrani, V., Jean-Gilles, M. and Szapocznik, J. (1997) 'Brief structural/strategic family therapy with African American and Hispanic high risk youth.' *Journal of Community Psychology 25,* 453–471.

Santisteban, D. A., Coatsworth, J. D., Perez-Vidal, A., Kurtines, W. M., Schwartz, S. J., LaPerriere, A. and Szapocznik, J. (2003) 'Efficacy of brief strategic family therapy in modifying Hispanic adolescent behavior problems and substance use.' *Journal of Family Psychology 17,* 1, 121–133.

Schaeffer, C. M., Petras, H., Ialongo, N., Poduska, J. and Kellam, S. (2003) 'Modeling growth in boys' aggressive behavior across elementary school: links to later criminal involvement, conduct disorder, and antisocial personality disorder.' *Developmental Psychology 39,* 6, 1020–1035.

Schoenwald, S. K., Halliday-Boykins, C. A. and Henggeler, S. W. (2003) 'Client-level predictors of adherence to MST in community service settings.' *Family Process 42,* 3, 345–359.

Schweinhart, L. J. and Weikart, D. P. (1980) *Young Children Grow Up: The Effects of the Perry Preschool Program on Youths Through Age 15.* Ypsilanti, MI: High/Scope Educational Research Foundation, p.7.

Scott, S., Knapp, M., Henderson, J. and Maughan, B. (2001) 'Financial cost of social exclusion: follow up study of antisocial children into adulthood.' *British Medical Journal 323,* 191.

Shamsie, J., Hamilton, H. and Sykes, C. (1996) 'The characteristics and intervention histories of incarcerated and conduct-disordered youth.' *Canadian Journal of Psychiatry 41,* 211–216.

Shepard, S. A. and Chamberlain, P. (2005) 'The Oregon multidimensional treatment foster care model. Research, community applications, and future directions.' In M. H. Epstein, K. Kutash and A. J. Duchnowski (eds) *Outcomes for Children and Youth with Emotional and Behavioral Disorders and Their Families. Programs and Evaluation Best Practices,* second edition. Austin, TX: Pro-ed.

Smith, D. J. (1995) 'Youth crime and conduct disorders: trends, patterns, and causal explanations.' In M. Rutter and D. J. Smith (eds) *Psychosocial Disorders in Young People. Time Trends and Their Causes.* Chichester: John Wiley and Sons Ltd, pp.389–489.

Smith, P. K., Ananiadou, K. and Cowie, H. (2003) 'Interventions to reduce school bullying.' *Canadian Journal of Psychiatry 48,* 591–599.

Smith, P. K. and Sharp, S. (1994) *School Bullying: Insights and Perspectives.* London: Routledge.

Snyder, J., Reid, J. and Patterson, G. (2003) 'A social learning model of child and adolescent antisocial behavior.' In B. B. Lahey, T. E. Moffitt and A. Caspi (eds) *Causes of Conduct Disorder and Juvenile Delinquency.* New York: The Guilford Press, pp.27–48.

Social Exclusion Unit (1998) *Truancy and School Exclusion.* London: The Social Exclusion Unit.

Spender, Q. and Scott, S. (1996) 'Conduct disorder.' *Current Opinion in Psychiatry 9,* 273–277.

Spitzer, R. L., Davies, M. and Barclay, R. (1991) 'The DSM-III-R field trials for the disruptive behavior disorders.' *Journal of American Academy of Child and Adolescent Psychiatry 29,* 1089–1102.

Stage, S. A. and Quiroz, D. R. (1997) 'A meta-analysis of interventions to decrease disruptive classroom behavior in public education settings.' *School Psychology Review 26,* 3, 333–368.

Stahl, N. D. and Clarizio, H. F. (1999) 'Conduct disorder and comorbidity.' *Psychology in the Schools 36,* 41–50.

Stanley, N., Riordan, D. and Alaszewski, H. (2005) 'The mental health of looked after children: matching response to need.' *Health and Social Care in the Community 13,* 3, 239–248.

Steiner, H., Saxena, K. and Chang, K. (2003) 'Psychopharmacologic strategies for the treatment of aggression in juveniles.' *CNS Spectrums 8,* 4, 1.

Steiner, H. and Wilson, J. (1999) 'Conduct disorder.' In R. L. Hendren (ed.) *Disruptive Behavior Disorders in Children and Adolescents*, vol. 18. Washington DC: American Psychiatric Press, pp.47–98.

Stevens, V., De Bourdeaudhuij, I. and Van Oost, P. (2001) 'Anti-bullying interventions at school: aspects of programme adaptation and critical issues for further programme development.' *Health Promotion International 16*, 2, 155–167.

Stouthamer-Loeber, M., Wei, E., Loeber, R. and Masten, A. (2004) 'Desistance from persistent serious delinquency in the transition to adulthood.' *Development and Psychopathology 16*, 4, Fal-918.

Sukhodolsky, D. G., Kassinove, H. and Gorman, B. S. (2004) 'Cognitive-behavioral therapy for anger in children and adolescents: a meta-analysis.' *Aggression and Violent Behaviour 9*, 247–269.

Sutton, C. (2002) *Protecting Children from Becoming Offenders: What Does the Evidence Suggest?* Leicester: Unit for Parenting Studies, De Montfort University.

Szapocznik, J., Rio, A., Murray, E., Cohen, R., Scopetta, M., Rivas-Valquez, A., Hervis, O., Posada, V. and Kurtines, W. M. (1989) 'Structural family versus psychodynamic child therapy for problematic Hispanic boys.' *Journal of Consulting and Clinical Psychology 567*, 571–578.

Thomas, A., Chess, S. and Birch, H. G. (1968) *Temperament and Behaviour Disorders in Children*. New York: Universities Press.

Toren, P., Laor, N. and Weizman, A. (1998) 'Use of atypical neuroleptics in child and adolescent psychiatry.' *Journal of Clinical Psychiatry 59*, 12, 644–656.

Turner, W. and Macdonald, G. M. (2006) 'Treatment foster care for improving outcomes in children and young people (protocol).' *The Cochrane Library 2*.

Turner, W., Macdonald, G. M. and Dennis, J. A. (2005) 'Cognitive-behavioural training interventions for assisting foster carers in the management of difficult behaviour (review).' *The Cochrane Library 4*, 1–30.

van de Wiel, N. M., Matthys, W., Cohen-Kettenis, P. and van Engeland, H. (2003) 'Application of the Utrecht Coping Power Program and care as usual to children with disruptive behavior disorders in outpatient clinics: a comparative study of cost and course of treatment.' *Behavior Therapy 34*, 421–436.

van der Wal, M., de Wit, C. A. M. and Hirasing, R. A. (2003) 'Psychosocial health among young victims and offenders of direct and indirect bullying.' *Pediatrics 111*, 6, 1312–1317.

van Manen, T. G., Prins, P. J. and Emmelkamp, P. M. (2004) 'Reducing aggressive behavior in boys with a social cognitive group treatment: results of a randomized, controlled trial.' *Journal of the American Academy of Child and Adolescent Psychiatry 43*, 12, 1478–1487.

Wadsworth, M. (1979) *Roots of Delinquency, Infancy, Adolescence and Crime*. Oxford: Robertson.

Wagman Borowsky, I., Mozayeny, S., Stuenkel, K. and Ireland, M. (2004) 'Effects of a primary care-based intervention on violent behavior and injury in children.' *Pediatrics 114*, 392–399.

Wakschlag, L. S., Lahey, B. B., Loeber, R., Green, S. M., Gordon, R. A. and Leventhal, B. L. (1997) 'Maternal smoking during pregnancy and the risk of conduct disorder in boys.' *Archives of General Psychiatry 54*, 670–676.

Walker, J. L., Lahey, B. B., Russo, M. F. and Frick, P. J. (1991) 'Anxiety, inhibition, and conduct disorder in children: I. Relations to social impairment.' *Journal of American Academy of Child and Adolescent Psychiatry 30*, 187–191.

Weisz, J. R., Hawley, K. M. and Doss, A. J. (2004) 'Empirically tested psychotherapies for youth internalizing and externalizing problems and disorders.' *Child and Adolescent Psychiatric Clinics of North America 13*, 4, 729–815.

Welsh, B. C. and Hoshi, A. (2002) 'Communities and crime prevention.' In L. W. Sherman, D. Farrington, B. C. Welsh and D. Layton MacKenzie (eds) *Evidence-based Crime Prevention*. London: Routledge, pp.165–197.

Werner, E. E. and Smith, R. S. (1982) *Vulnerable But Invincible: A Study of Resilient Children*. New York: McGraw-Hill.

Werry, J. S. (1997) 'Severe conduct disorder – some key issues.' *Canadian Journal of Psychiatry 42*, 577–583.

White, J. L., Moffitt, T. E., Earls, F., Robins, L. and Silva, P. A. (2004) 'How early can we tell? Predictors of childhood conduct disorder and adolescent delinquency.' *Criminology 28*, 4, 507–533.

WHO (1994) *ICD-10: International Statistical Classification of Diseases and Related Health Problems: Tenth Revision.* (Second edition) Geneva: World Health Organization.

Willcutt, E. G., Pennington, B. F., Chhabildas, N. A., Friedman, M. C. and Alexander, J. (1999) 'Psychiatric comorbidity associated with DSM-IV ADHD in a nonreferred sample of twins.' *American Academy of Child and Adolescent Psychiatry 38*, 1355–1362.

Wilson, D. B., MacKenzie, D. L. and Mitchell, F. N. (2005) *Effects of Correctional Boot Camps on Offending. A Campbell Collaboration Systematic Review.* Available at: www.aic.gov.au/campbellcj/reviews/titles.html.

Wilson, S. J. and Lipsey, M. W. (2000) 'Wilderness challenge programs for delinquency youth: a meta-analysis of outcome evaluations.' *Evaluation and Program Planning 2*, 3, 1–12.

Wilson, S. J. and Lipsey, M. W. (2006a) *The Effects of School-based Social Information Processing Programs on Aggressive Behavior: Part I: Universal Programs.* Campbell Collaboration Systematic Review.

Wilson, S. J. and Lipsey, M. W. (2006b) *The Effects of School-based Social Information Processing Interventions on Aggressive Behavior: Part II: Selected/Indicated Pull-out Programs.* Campbell Collaboration Systematic Review.

Wilson, S. J., Lipsey, M. W. and Soydan, H. (2003) 'Are mainstream programs for juvenile delinquency less effective with minority youth than majority youth? A meta-analysis of outcomes research.' *Research on Social Work Practice 13*, 1, 3–26.

Wolpert, M., Fuggle, P., Cottrell, D., Fonagy, P., Phillips, J., Pilling, S., Stein, S. and Target, M. (2006) *Drawing on the Evidence. Advice for Mental Health Professionals Working with Children and Adolescents.* London: CAMHS Evidence-Based Practice Unit.

Wood, M. (2005) *The Victimisation of Young People: Findings from the Crime and Justice Survey 2003.* London: The Research, Development and Statistics Directorate, Findings 246.

Woolfenden, S. R., Williams, K. and Peat, J. K. (2001) 'Family and parenting interventions for conduct disorder and delinquency in children aged 10–17.' *Cochrane Database of Systematic Reviews.*

Woolfenden, S. R., Williams, K. and Peat, J. K. (2002) 'Family and parenting interventions for conduct disorder and delinquency: a meta-analysis of randomised controlled trials.' *Archives of Disease in Childhood 86*, 251–256.

Yoshikawa, H. (1994) 'Prevention as cumulative protection: effects of early family support and education on chronic delinquency and its risks.' *Psychological Bulletin 15*, 1, 28–54.

Youth Justice Board (2003) *Key Elements of Effective Practice. Mental Health.* London: YJB.

Youth Justice Board (2004) *National Standards for Youth Justice Services.* London: YJB.

Youth Justice Board (2006) *Asset.* London: YJB.

Zoccolillo, M. (1992) 'Co-occurrence of conduct disorder and its adult outcomes with depressive and anxiety disorders: a review.' *Journal of the American Academy of Child and Adolescent Psychiatry 31*, 547–556.

Subject Index

Author Index

About FOCUS

FOCUS was launched in 1997 to promote clinical and organisational effectiveness in child and adolescent mental health services, with an emphasis on incorporating evidence-based research into everyday practice.

Please visit our website to find out more about our work (including our discussion forum and conferences): www.rcpsych.ac.uk/crtu/focus.aspx